Supporting the W
Children with SE

As an early years practitioner, you will educate and care for children with a range of developmental needs and differences. This essential book introduces you to a play-rich approach providing both universal and targeted ideas that will support social and emotional development and ensure that children feel safe, secure and nurtured.

Using the four broad areas of need as a guide, each accessible chapter positions wellbeing at the heart of an effective approach to inclusion and offers meaningful and responsive teaching practices that create a sense of belonging and acceptance. Founded in the latest research, the book presents key knowledge alongside ideas and activities to support wellbeing, which can be embedded into the child's everyday experiences and adapted to meet their individual needs.

This book offers:

- Evidence-based strategies and techniques that have a positive impact on the long-term social and emotional wellbeing of children with SEND.
- Guidance through the four broad areas of need, with a focus on play, learning, and developing an emotionally healthy early years environment.
- Examples of practice in action.
- Case studies, reflective questions, and activities that will upskill the reader and empower them in their role.

Providing up to date, transferrable and essential knowledge on SEND in the early years, this is an essential resource for any practitioner looking to expand their repertoire and enrich the wellbeing of children with SEND.

Kerry Murphy is an early years specialist in special educational needs, disability and development differences. She adopts a pro-neurodiversity framework and currently works as a lecturer in early education and SEN. She is also an independent trainer and consultant. Kerry worked in a local authority for six years, developing strategic links between early education, health and social care. She is an associate for early education and has written for national organisations including Nursery World and Teach Early Years. Kerry is also studying towards her doctorate in early intervention.

Little Minds Matter: Promoting Social and Emotional Wellbeing in the Early Years

Series Advisor: Sonia Mainstone-Cotton

The *Little Minds Matter* series promotes best practice for integrating social and emotional health and wellbeing into the early years setting. It introduces practitioners to a wealth of activities and resources to support them in each key area: from providing access to ideas for unstructured, imaginative outdoor play; activities to create a sense of belonging and form positive identities; and, importantly, strategies to encourage early years professionals to create a workplace that positively contributes to their own wellbeing, as well as the quality of their provision. The *Little Minds Matter* series ensures that practitioners have the tools they need to support every child.

Outdoor Play for Healthy Little Minds
Practical Ideas to Promote Children's Wellbeing in the Early Years
Sarah Watkins

Supporting the Wellbeing of Children with SEND
Essential Ideas for Early Years Educators
Kerry Murphy

A Guide to Mental Health for Early Years Educators
Putting Wellbeing at the Heart of Your Philosophy and Practice
Kate Moxley

Supporting the Wellbeing of Children with SEND

Essential Ideas for Early Years Educators

Kerry Murphy

Routledge
Taylor & Francis Group

LONDON AND NEW YORK

Cover image: Robin is one and a half years old and has social communication differences and sensory processing issues. He is a sensory seeker, and to create this painting he used his hands and vehicles, as he loves creating tracks.

First published 2022
by Routledge
4 Park Square, Milton Park, Abingdon, Oxon OX14 4RN

and by Routledge
605 Third Avenue, New York, NY 10158

Routledge is an imprint of the Taylor & Francis Group, an informa business

© 2022 Kerry Murphy

The right of Kerry Murphy to be identified as author of this work has been asserted in accordance with sections 77 and 78 of the Copyright, Designs and Patents Act 1988.

British Library Cataloguing-in-Publication Data
A catalogue record for this book is available from the British Library

Library of Congress Cataloging-in-Publication Data
A catalog record has been requested for this book

ISBN: 978-0-367-68636-9 (hbk)
ISBN: 978-0-367-68635-2 (pbk)
ISBN: 978-1-003-13836-5 (ebk)

DOI: 10.4324/9781003138365

Typeset in Optima
by Deanta Global Publishing Services, Chennai, India

Contents

Foreword

This latest book in the Little Minds Matter series is on wellbeing and SEND. We don't often hear or read about these two topics together, so I am thrilled to have this important book as part of our series. Supporting wellbeing is crucial for all children and adults; however, not all the proposed, mainstream strategies – advocated by many – work for all. In this book, Kerry shares ideas and knowledge around how we can expand and adapt our approach to meet the specific needs of the individual child.

Kerry has a wealth of experience and knowledge in this area; it was fantastic to read her insights and reflections. So often, we can view SEND through a narrow and negative lens, but Kerry shines a light on this negative thinking, unravelling common misunderstandings and challenging the reader to view SEND through a different framework.

Kerry's book blends a mix of current theory and practice from across various settings and features a range of early years voices, sharing a wide variety of experiences and examples. The book explores an array of SEND topics that many early years practitioners will encounter with children. Often practitioners can feel overwhelmed by SEND areas; however, Kerry successfully unpicks them, explains them, and weaves in wellbeing practice throughout.

It feels so timely to be publishing this book. Kerry reminds us that when we think about wellbeing practice, we need to pay particular attention to how we can ensure our children with SEND also have good wellbeing and mental health. As early years practitioners, we play an essential part in embedding excellent wellbeing practices and strategies for all our children.

I took away many new ideas, thoughts and reflections from reading this book. I am sure you will too.

Sonia Mainstone-Cotton
Series Advisor
May 2021

Preface

You wouldn't be mistaken to think that wellbeing is a hot topic right now in the early years sector. It seems that everyone is invested in an emotionally tuned-in pedagogy, but given that the sector continues to face a mental health crisis for staff (Minds Matter, 2018) and children (Lancet, 2020), it begs the question, why isn't our increased knowledge leading to the transformation of practice? A global pandemic has been particularly devastating, but it has also brought to the surface the deep-rooted inequalities and injustices that have long existed within our sector. While this book is not a pandemic recovery guide, much of what will be covered will be underpinned by these inequalities and the lack of equity in wellbeing, particularly for children with special educational needs, disabilities and neurodivergence. Other identity markers such as race, class and gender will also be covered. It is particularly pertinent to point out that people with a medically diagnosed learning disability have been disproportionately affected by COVID-19, and the risk of death is 3.7 times greater than people without a learning disability (Office for National Statistics, 2020).

I was reluctant to begin this book on such a bleak note, but it is vital to acknowledge that wellbeing and well-doing exist upon all children's fundamental rights to feel safe, protected, and free from harm. While I fully advocate and embrace the importance of wellbeing, it is essential to recognise that as a concept, it is much messier and complex than standard acts of commercialised self care, mindful breathing and yoga poses – though these all do add to our good practice too.

This book is a timely exploration of wellbeing for those children that do not fit neatly into the narrow definitions of development and whose needs cannot necessarily be met by universal co and self-regulation strategies. Research and anecdotal examples of our practice in action tell us that if children are not supported to develop their social and emotional worlds, this can lead to poor mental health. One quick Google search will clearly illustrate the long-term impact of mental health difficulties in childhood and how it can impede long-term life outcomes (DfE, 2016), but we must also be mindful of the "headlines" and some of the harmful underlying messages that can emerge about why mental health becomes an issue, particularly those that place blame or reinforce stereotypes.

For example, despite increased focus on the importance of wellbeing, access to support is still varied and inequitable and even though we know mental health difficulties emerge in early childhood, there is limited specialist support from mental health professionals or services. At the time of writing, the Child and Adolescent Mental Health Services (CAMHS) still do not accept referrals for children under 5 years of age. I mention this due to the ongoing emphasis that early intervention is best and is most effective for reducing health inequalities (Allen, 2011). An independent review stated that early intervention should be placed at the heart of education and that high-quality provision is essential for younger children. For many of us currently working within the sector, I think we have lots of questions about how well that heart is beating regarding the effectiveness and accessibility of early intervention. What are we left with if support services are not firmly and consistently in place?

As we will come on to see, much of what we know as educators comes from our everyday lived experiences with children and with families. There is an ongoing absence for training and professional development, and so this leaves us in a bit of a quandary – how can we provide high-quality provision for wellbeing if we are not equipped with the tools to do so? While this book will not solve that quandary, it is undoubtedly designed to be something you can access and use to build upon your practice, and its aim is to give you some starting points and springboards to make wellbeing, well-becoming and well-doing work within your setting. We need to ensure that in our quest for inclusion, we do not get consumed by buzzwords and tokenistic practices, but rather we need to deeply understand the diversity of wellbeing. According to Devarakonda (2012), we hear a lot of discussion based on diversity, removing barriers, equality of opportunity and celebrating differences, but these things mean different things to different people, and it is our role as educators to be culturally responsive, sensitive and flexible in meeting these aims.

Language and terminology

The language of inclusion can become tricky and complicated. For this book, I have made several decisions regarding language and terminology:

1. As a neurodivergent author, I believe that a person's disability is central to their identity. I have decided to use identity-first language throughout these chapters. For example, autistic child as opposed to child with autism.
2. To describe a person in the early years, I have used the terminology "educator" as I believe this is the most appropriate umbrella term for someone who provides caregiving and education. This term includes practitioners, teachers, childminders and specialists.
3. Special educational needs is the commonly used terminology in the 0–25 Special Educational Needs & Disability (SEND) Code of Practice (DfE, 2015) and is a familiar term to most educators. It has rightly been contested as an unhelpful way to describe children with developmental needs and can reinforce stereotypes and discrimination. It is used here as an officially recognised term, but the author recognises that our language will move on over time.
4. I actively avoid using the term "disorder" and prefer to describe neurodivergence as a condition or difference. The term "disorder" can imply that differences are wholly deficit and negative, and as many people will know, SEND includes many positive traits and strengths.
5. The formal term for early intervention is SEN support, but I use the term SEND support to account for those with a disability. However, the processes remain the same.

6. There will be points throughout this book that I will not directly link the topic back to wellbeing. The reader should go on the assumption that everything I write is with wellbeing in mind.

7. Knowledge and understanding of SEND are constantly evolving. Therefore, some of my perspectives may become outdated or develop after the book has been published. Always check how up to date a view may be and consolidate this to ensure that the application to practice remains appropriate.

1 | Introducing wellbeing and SEND

Starting points

Before we begin, it is essential to reflect on the language of wellbeing and SEND. According to researchers, the term "social and emotional wellbeing" is often used instead of "mental health." This is potentially due to the stigma of perceived mental illness (Frederickson, Dunsmuir and Baxter, 2009). However, the 0–25 SEND Code of Practice (DfE, 2015) clearly outlines social, emotional and/or mental health (SEMH) as a broad area of need. Educators should be alert to emerging concerns within this area. While some children will have SEMH as an immediate and distinct need, it is not uncommon for other types of SEND to co-exist with SEMH needs. As a starting point, consider the following reflections:

What are your thoughts on mental health terminology?

Do you feel comfortable talking about the different components of mental health, including social and emotional wellbeing?

Why do you think it is vital to establish a shared consensus on the language of mental health and wellbeing?

Introduction

One of the most important messages throughout this book is that childhood takes time and is not a race to some imaginary finish line. Magda Gerber states, *"Earlier is not better. All children accomplish milestones*

DOI: 10.4324/9781003138365-1

in their own way in their own time." Learning and development is a lifelong pursuit, and children need our availability, advocacy and love for learning. Children are competent and far more capable than we often realise, and this fact remains true when we think about children who have special educational needs and disabilities (SEND).

The result of an educators work should be to provide a springboard for children to thrive, but we must acknowledge that the concept of thriving is diverse and its meaning will vary. In the early years, we are often told to meet children where they are and to scaffold up their learning and development appropriately. We will build upon this fundamental principle within these pages and consider how we can do this effectively for children with SEND who can become overlooked when we think about play, learning, development and wellbeing. SEND support is so often dominated by paperwork, planning and procedures that time to actually implement holistic support can become disrupted. And so, this book will encourage you to prioritise time with children and to expand your repertoire of knowledge, skills and strategies so that you can fully support wellbeing and thriving in a personalised way.

You will notice many different chapter features that will make this an easy "dip-in-and-out" book, particularly if you are looking for ideas, activities and strategies for children's wellbeing. When you utilise these strategies, it is essential that they are embedded into the child's everyday experiences and adapted to meet individual needs. On their own, they can become tokenistic, and so throughout the book, you will have opportunities to think about how you can build celebratory profiles for your children with SEND. Things to look out for across the chapters:

- Reflections and activities

    There are individual and collective points in which you can consider your current practice and areas of development. These would be useful in team meetings or virtual CPD sessions.

- Research snippets and "Did you know?"

    There are lots of examples of research for you to consider when developing your approach to wellbeing. It is important to remember that our understanding and evidence-base evolves, so "hold your knowledge lightly" and be open to adaptations in practice as we come to understand more about SEND and wellbeing. There are also "Did you know?" boxes that challenge some of our current perceptions around SEND.

- Wellbeing strategies and strategies to avoid

  Throughout the book, you will see lots of evidence-based and anecdotal strategies. You must think about these in the context of children's everyday experiences and play. There are also strategies to avoid due to being ineffective, controversial or harmful to wellbeing and mental health.

- Case studies and "voice"

  The chapter includes examples of real case studies that will help you develop your practice and children's, families and professionals' "voices" because all perspectives count.

- Read, watch and listen

  At the end of each chapter, you will find signposts to other resources for your professional development. These signposts will help you to strengthen your practice.

- The wellbeing scales

  Also included in the book is the scales symbol. This will be a moment for you to reflect on the risk and protective factors that can tip the wellbeing scales. We will discuss these in more detail across this chapter.

Defining SEND and inclusion in the early years

Before we consider the formal definition of SEND, we should acknowledge the Early Years Foundation Stage (DfE, 2021), which states that all children are unique, constantly learning and that learning occurs in different ways. The child should be centred as competent and capable, and we should view SEND through a strengths-based approach. The image below places the child at the centre of a hierarchy of good practices, and as we progress through this book, the different levels will become further contextualised.

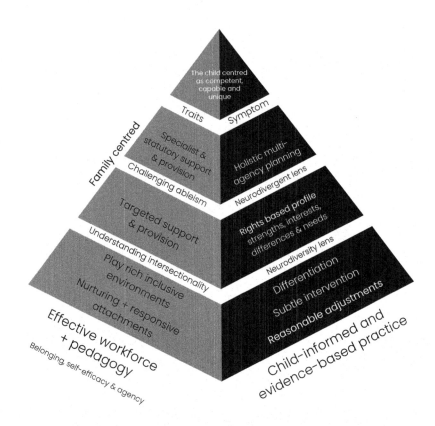

The 0–25 SEND Code of Practice (DfE, 2015) provides a general definition of SEN, but as you will see, it is relatively basic and doesn't necessarily provide a holistic description:

- A child or young person has SEN if they have a learning difficulty or disability, which calls for special educational provisions to be made for him or her.
- A child of compulsory school age or a young person has a learning difficulty or disability if he or she:
  - has significantly greater difficulty in learning than the majority of others of the same age, or

* has a disability that prevents or hinders him or her from making use of facilities of a kind generally provided for others of the same age in mainstream schools or mainstream post-16 institutions

(SEND Code of Practice: 0–25, 2015, p. 16)

As you will have noticed, the current definition is aimed at children of compulsory school age. Within our everyday practice, we are required to anticipate whether a child would fall under this definition by the time they enter compulsory education. It is also important to acknowledge that special educational needs and disabilities can require transient or permanent support, and similarly all children may have specific needs at different points (Sandberg et al., 2010). Generally, however, the definitions of disability are much broader than educators realise. Disability is defined under the Equality Act (EqA) (2010) as;

a physical or mental impairment that has a 'substantial' and 'long-term' negative effect on your ability to do normal daily activities.

It is vital to be aware that the EqA (2010) has a wider coverage of nine protected characteristics include disability, gender and ethnicity. (A detailed guide can be found under "Read, watch and listen" in Chapter 1)

Is the term SEND fit for purpose?

Another discussion point in research is that the term SEND can imply that the child is a burden because they require something additional to or separate from the everyday provision. According to Kathryn Underwood (2019),

> thinking about some children as part of a special group who have particular needs reinforces a discriminatory system. There are better ways to talk about the diversity of children's abilities that recognise the wide variance in all children's development, emotions, mental outlooks, physical capabilities, communication, and social worlds – all of which exist for all children whether someone has diagnosed these differences as special or not.
>
> (College of Early Childhood Educators, 2019)

Neurodiversity model

Edward Hallowell once remarked to his daughter that "No brain is the same; no brain is best. Each brain finds its own special way." As educators, it is important that we develop a practice that really embraces and acknowledges that developmental differences aren't necessarily a bad thing, in fact, they can become a competitive advantage (Austin & Pisano, 2017). It is believed that neurodiversity was coined by autism activist Judy Singer in the 1990s and is short for neurological diversity – or differences in the brain. It is an approach and movement you may have heard of, particularly within the autistic community, which challenges the idea that neurodevelopmental differences are abnormal and need to be cured (Understood.org). Within neurodiversity, some individuals follow a typical development trajectory, referred to as neurotypical, while those whose development diverges are called neurodivergent. Neurotypes include autism, ADHD and dyslexia, to name a few. Many developmental conditions, however, have negative associations because they do not fit into a neurotypical worldview. The neurodiversity movement encourages people to embrace living, learning and viewing the world differently. This is important, especially for neurodivergent people who have always been made to believe that they must change to fit society's expectations. Sadly, these negative beliefs can emerge in early childhood and impede children's daily activities, motivation and behaviours. Ultimately, when we view developmental differences as entirely negative, it can impact children's self-esteem and self-perception (Saigal et al., 2002), and our feedback to children about their differences can also influence identity and wellbeing.

So, the most crucial question for early years educators is: what influence do you want to have? I spoke with a SENCO who noticed that key people would often talk openly in front of children about their delays, such as during the handover with parents, and she did a lot of training and mentoring with her team about embracing strengths, differences, interests and needs. A meaningful discussion that arose during these sessions addressed that neurodiversity does not ignore the difficulties a child may have but instead views the child's development much more holistically and acknowledges that society can exacerbate these difficulties. I often encourage educators to take a neurodiversity affirming approach, which means to support the individuals' unique characteristics and traits and use these as a springboard for development. Our role is to help shape a child's identity and sense of self, and so we must find ways to affirm rather than reject who they are.

Inclusion

According to Tedam (2013), "All children have a right to inclusion in the main-stream education system. The implementation of inclusion goes through a never-ending process of breaking down barriers to participation" (p. 11). And so, one of the critical ideas to explore when we think of SEND is whether our practice and pedagogy is inclusive of all children. A key question I ask educators is whether they welcome the complexity of what children bring to our settings and do those children see themselves as woven into the fabric of our provision. It may be an uncomfortable reflection to have, but the reality is that there are many examples of children not being accepted to a setting based on their identified needs. For example, in my local authority role, settings would often turn down places with-out first assessing whether they could actually make the adaptation and adjust-ments for a disabled child. When I spoke to settings, they would often say that it was not their job to meet such a broad range of needs. It was often made harder to challenge this when the framework we have in place does not more clearly describe neurodivergent and disabled learning and development. One of the barriers of the EYFS (DfE, 2021) is that it does not define diversity within develop-ment very well, and the narrow developmental statements can lead to educators viewing SEND as outside their remit. Equally, educators can often feel frustrated that they are ill-equipped to support the ever-increasing needs of children with SEND, often with little access to support. This is a genuine problem within the early years and education sector, making it harder for a child to be fully accepted.

The reality is that lack of inclusion is not always the fault of the set-ting but is more a fundamental issue with the systems and structures of early years' provision. Nutbrown et al. (2013) have written extensively about inclusion and encourages us to think of it as an active and ongoing process. Along the way, we will encounter both positive and challenging factors in our quest to include everyone, but the key is to develop anticipatory and reflective practices that help us to make decisions that are in the best inter-ests of the child. These opportunities for overcoming challenges ultimately improve our practice and provision. According to UNICEF (2017), inclusion is a process in which we identify and address the diverse needs of our chil-dren and families, with the primary goal being participation. Think of this from your own perspective, and how it might feel if you were not heard or understood, or if you were excluded from experiences. For a child with SEND, this experience can directly impact their wellbeing, which ultimately can reduce their participation and motivation in learning.

Defining wellbeing

The scales of wellbeing

Despite the growing popularity and appeal of wellbeing practices in the early years, subjective wellbeing is a hard term to define. Researchers have found it hard to conceptualise its exact meaning in early childhood (Lewis, 2019). There is no universally recognised definition of child wellbeing with researchers arguing that this lack of understanding "stems from the dominant and long-standing view of children as merely future adults, who, as a result, do not require a theory of their own" (Raghavan and Alexandrova, 2015, p. 893). However, the consensus is that it is a holistic and multi-dimensional concept influenced by many different factors, including culture, experience and values. In short, wellbeing will mean different things to different people and may require educators to engage in possibilities beyond their own frame of reference. Dodge et al. (2012) describe a person's wellbeing as a set of scales which need to be balanced to create stability. They state that "stable wellbeing is when individuals have the psychological, social and physical resources they need to meet a particular psychological, social or physical challenge. When individuals have more challenges than resources, the (scales) dip, along with their wellbeing and vice-versa" (p. 230).

Visualising wellbeing in this way is helpful because we can acknowledge that balance is not always possible. Daily events and experiences can tip our scales depending on our individual experiences. The idea is that our scales are in a continual state of flux, and therefore always

Wellbeing scales

The aim is to keep the scales balanced for wellbeing

A trusted adult can help maintain balance

Protective factors

Risk factors

influenced by inner experiences, relationships and environmental factors. It also helps to think about those children or adults who constantly have their scales tipped, for example, children who have experienced trauma, discrimination or have unmet SEND needs.

RESEARCH SNIPPETS

Read the following research snippets and consider the questions

- According to Ereaut and Whiting (2008), the definition of wellbeing is not fixed and is primarily a cultural judgement.
- Similarly, Gasper (2010) states that wellbeing is not a single definitive thing. He describes wellbeing as "fuzzy" and contingent on lots of different things, meaning its definition varies from person to person.

  In what ways do you learn about what wellbeing means to different children, families and colleagues?

- According to Mashford-Scott et al. (2012), wellbeing is often described as a "catch-all" concept and is therefore often misunderstood. There is no consensus among cultures, languages and disciplines, so we must be mindful of projecting our own definition onto others.

  Why do you think it is important not to project our ideas of wellbeing onto others?

  How do we develop a culturally sensitive and curious response to differences in wellbeing?

- Wellbeing is often linked to happiness, quality of life, emotional literacy and emotional intelligence, and this can lead people to think that wellbeing is the absence of adversity or mental illness. There can also be an assumption that wellbeing needs to be done the "right way," but it is a subjective concept, and we need to be sensitive to differences within wellbeing.

  Do you ever feel pressure to do wellbeing the "right way"? How does this make you feel?

ACTIVITY

If wellbeing is a highly subjective and unique experience, it will be important for a setting to consider the current cohort of children and families' needs and to be flexible within their practice. Try the following:

- As a team, discuss what child wellbeing means to each of you and create a collaborative definition.
- Using ⚖ the wellbeing scales, can you think of any examples of why the scales might tip? And how might this throw a child's wellbeing off balance? What might we do to restore the balance? Throughout this book, we will return to the idea of how we can balance out the wellbeing scales in practice.

Wellbeing pedagogy

While its presence in the early years grows, there is also the real risk of some wellbeing practices becoming quite tokenistic or narrow. For example, when I spoke with early years educators, key terms kept emerging, such as self-care, happiness, yoga and breathing. In short, it appeared that educators' understanding remained very much at a surface level. When I further explored wellbeing and SEND, there was even less understanding about what this might look like in our everyday practice. Because wellbeing is subjective it is not useful to be tied to a single definition (White and Abeyasekera, 2014), but instead to consider key features that describe and contribute to wellbeing, well-becoming and well-doing. Using the visual below, discuss with your team where you currently feel you are at with developing a wellbeing pedagogy. The examples listed below may differ from your own, so the most important thing to explore is how deep your understanding of wellbeing is.

Surface wellbeing	Breathing exercises
	Yoga Calm down corners
	Behaviour management

Shallow wellbeing	Labelling core feelings
	Emotional literacy Behaviour supports

Deep wellbeing	Emotional co-regulation
	Safety and security Differentiated strategies
	Professional love Consistency Creativity
	Moving through moods
	Sensory diet
	Emotional intelligence Stressors Communication
	understood preferences
	Representative Independence understood &
	emotional reciprocated
	literacy Inclusion

We must consider how inclusive our setting is when we think about well-being. The purpose of exploring surface wellbeing is to acknowledge that universal strategies such as yoga or having books about feelings will not necessarily suit all children's stages of social and emotional development. We must go much deeper and develop a repertoire of strategies underpinned by a strong understanding of social, emotional and mental health.

The core needs of flourishing

Wendy Ellyatt, the founder of the Save Childhood Movement, developed the Flourish model (2019) to describe children's need for an emotionally healthy and rights-based childhood. She describes this model as dynamic and non-linear, recognising that child development is neither a straightforward nor a narrow process. Our developmental experiences are shaped by the "right relationships" (p. 2), where we grow into our values, wellbeing, beliefs and mindset. The concern, however, is that we currently exist within a high-stakes education system that places far too much emphasis on rote teaching and recall of knowledge rather than supporting lifelong learning dispositions. This she fears has led to real neglect of the idea of "developing well" (p. 2) in childhood, and without this essential foundation in place, maintaining wellbeing both individually and collectively will become very challenging. Ellyatt contextualises wellbeing through five aspects:

1. Early Wellbeing (Developing Well)
2. Personal Wellbeing (Living Well)
3. Community Wellbeing (Living Well Locally)
4. Societal Wellbeing (Living Well Together)
5. Planetary Wellbeing (Living Well Sustainably)

(The Ecology of Wellbeing, 2020)

ACTIVITY

Using the full document, how do these aspects show up in your everyday practice? Can you think of examples from each? How embedded are they within the culture of your everyday setting?

In addition to the aspects of wellbeing, Ellyatt also describes the seven core needs of flourishing that she considers central to wellbeing:

Flourishing consists of...

HUMAN NEEDS

NO MATTER WHERE CHILDREN LIVE IN THE WORLD THEY ALL HAVE THE SAME CORE NEEDS

To flourish all children need their physical, emotional, mental and spiritual needs met.

And so do the adults who help shape their identity.

SPIRITUAL
- GROWTH — Expansion and vitality
- CONTRIBUTION — Empathy and co-operation

MENTAL
- FULFILMENT — Self-expression and achievement
- ENGAGEMENT — Meaning-making and flow

EMOTIONAL
- INDEPENDENCE — Mastery and self-worth
- RELATIONSHIP — Nurturing relationships

PHYSICAL
- SECURITY — Nurturing environments

It is important that we consider these human needs through an intersectional lens, and reflect upon what these might "look" like for children with SEND:

Need

Security

Children with SEND must feel safe and secure within their environment. Educators should aim to offer routines and rhythms that are predictable, familiar and which cultivate a sense of belonging. The environment acts as a secure base, springboard and safety net for play, learning and exploration.

Children feel secure because they have a sense of autonomy and agency within the environment and their "voice" informs how they are supported.

Relationships

Children with SEND must be in the presence of responsive adults who professionally love and understand them. Educators recognise that education and caregiving are deeply interconnected and together form the foundations for learning. Educators build resilience through positive experiences and co-regulate alongside the child when "bumps in the road" or challenges occur.

Educators understand that in caregiving, they are using the "good enough" approach to relationships recognising that it might take time to form attachments, and bonds, and that where a child has SEND, it may take longer to figure each other out. Educators remain aware of their bias toward children, and challenge perceptions that may disrupt attachments.

Independence

Children with SEND may have specific needs that include a higher level of dependence over a longer period, but knowledgeable educators support children through scaffolding up their learning and developing increasing independence. The environment is used as a "third teacher" to help guide and navigate children to increasing feelings of "I can do this myself."

Reasonable adjustments along with targeted and specialist support are used in a child-centred way, and decisions are made in the best interests of the child.

Engagement

Educators do not prescribe to the idea that there is only one way to play and learn, and children's interests, ideas and diverse ways of playing are embraced and understood through good observational attention. Children with SEND are given time and space to develop and thrive through play-rich approaches and child-led early intervention.

(Continued)

(Continued)

Need

Fulfilment

A child's SEND is not viewed through a deficit lens but is understood holistically. Children's emotions and feelings are embraced and welcomed; their emotional needs are met with consistency, adaptations and differentiation.

Contribution

The setting values a multi-modal and multi-sensory way of learning, and the perspectives of the child are fully considered. Children's ideas and ways of playing are acknowledged and celebrated, and there are opportunities to understand how children contribute to the setting community.

Growth

All educators understand the diversity within the development and actively celebrate the different types of learning and "milestones." Children's development isn't ringfenced because they have SEND or because their development doesn't fit neatly into narrow developmental statements.

Why wellbeing and SEND?

Four broad areas of need

Being invested in a child's social and emotional experiences is a fundamental aspect of early years practice. Educators should understand that good mental health forms solid foundations for development. Mojdeh Bayat (2019) suggests that when children have a good sense of wellbeing, this also translates into well-doing, meaning that children can access play and learning in a stress-free state. Worryingly, however, research also suggests that children with special educational needs and/or a disability (SEND) are at a higher risk of experiencing social, emotional and mental health difficulties (SEMH).

While the possible reasons for SEMH needs are vast, we must develop the skills and knowledge to unpick these reasons and their possible underlying causes. One of the ways to support children is to understand their inner worlds and experiences. We need a good understanding of the role of social, emotional and mental health in the early years, including how to identify and support SEMH, notably when it is co-existing with other

SEND needs. Interestingly, when speaking with early years educators on their knowledge of SEMH, they stated the following:

- "Behaviour for a typically developing child is difficult to support, so when there is the additional factor of SEND, it becomes even more complicated and hard to figure out."
- "It seems like such an important area for children's development but is the area in which we often feel least experienced."
- "Wellbeing has become such a buzzword, and it can be frustrating when the suggested answer to a child's social and emotional difficulties is to do some breathing or yoga. For this reason, I tend to find wellbeing as a topic quite annoying."
- "It sounds terrible, but it can feel like one thing on top of another, and when you have a child with SEND, it is difficult to know which area of need to address first. It is overwhelming."

In these initial discussions, the thing that stood out to me is that children's developmental domains were viewed as separate from each other, fragmented or disconnected, and that wellbeing was the afterthought. Under pressure from other demands, it appeared that it was difficult for wellbeing to be the starting point. All development domains are interconnected and dependent on each other, but good social, emotional and mental health levels are the foundation for all learning, engagement and wellbeing. In other words, you have to feel a sense of wellness to get involved in your play and learning. Without this, a child might feel withdrawn, disengaged, frustrated and unsupported. For a child with SEND, we must take additional steps to understand the ways to wellbeing and explore how we can ensure full participation in learning.

For this book, we will use the four broad areas of need (DfE, 2014) to guide our understanding of wellbeing. The four broad areas of need are

- Communication and interaction needs
- Cognition and learning needs
- Physical and/or sensory needs
- Social, emotional and/or mental health needs

(0–25 SEND Code of Practice, DfE, 2015)

When using the four broad areas, it is important to recognise that children's SEND needs aren't always so easily categorised, but they serve as a good way to organise our thinking and priorities. Educators often comment that many types of SEN and disabilities present with needs across the broad areas, so it is not uncommon to be supporting multiple needs at once. Usually, in an educational context, educators will identify primary and secondary needs and then focus their teaching, differentiation and provision according to these needs.

Intersectional needs

It is also crucial to consider the intersectional needs of children, as there are often other contextualising factors at play. According to the Good Practice Guidelines by the College of Early Childhood Educators (2020):

> Children with disabilities are not one uniform group. It is important to consider the various contexts and factors that shape a child's development and identity within their families and communities. These factors impact how children view themselves and their ability to participate and engage in their environment. For example, not all children with the same diagnosis have the same experiences with disability, nor do they have the same experiences in their home life, community, child care or school. Overlapping factors that might influence a child's lived experiences, like access to resources, are complex and varied. As a professional, you need to make yourself aware of the various and shifting contexts and factors that impact children with disabilities and their families.
>
> (p. 9)

Some of the factors to be aware of include race, ethnicity, ability, gender, socio-economic background and age. By developing a clear understanding of the impact these contextual factors can have, we can behave more sensitively to the lived experiences of children and families within our care. For example, boys are disproportionately diagnosed with developmental disabilities such as autism spectrum conditions compared to girls. While some arguments have suggested that this is a result of gender differences, a more significant question is whether girls are potentially being overlooked or misdiagnosed, leading to a much later identification of needs, and therefore a lack of appropriate early intervention (Leedham, Thompson, Smith and Freeth, 2020).

Intersectionality and privilege

Intersectionality describes the overlapping and interdependent systems of oppression across different characteristics, including race, gender, neurodiversity, economic background and age. Intersectionality highlights the complex relationship between these characteristics emphasising the interplay of privilege and discrimination. Intersectionality leads to the existence of "isms," for example, racism, classism, ageism, sexism and ableism (Derman-Sparks, Olsen-Edwards and Goins, 2017).

Look at the following characteristics below. Consider the ways in which you might feel privileged or discriminated in each area, for example, which of these do you think about often, and why, and which do you not give much thought to. Why do you think this is?:

Race	Gender	Education	Ethnicity
Sexuality	Immigration status	Language	Poverty and socio-economic status
Family structure	Culture	Location	Sex
Religion	Age	Disability	

You may look at this and quickly identify the ones that you feel judged by, because those experiences often feel much stronger, and there may be others that you don't even think about because of the absence of discriminatory experience. For example, people racialised as white may deny the existence of white privilege because they may have their own sets of struggles. Intersectionality is not about who wins at being discriminated against, its purpose is to highlight that the systems and structures within our society can further marginalise certain groups of people. This is of critical importance within SEND for a number of reasons that will be outlined below:

- It is within SEND that we see the intersection of bias against children of colour (Graham, 2019).

- Research suggests that children who fall outside of the realms of "ideal" (white, conformist and normative) are problematic for our education system (bias view).
- It is more common for children of colour, specifically Black Caribbean boys to be prematurely labelled (thus marginalised), misdiagnosed (this doesn't mean to say there isn't a diagnosis of some kind), to experience adultification bias and to become criminalised within practice.
- A PhD study in special education identified that black teachers were more likely to accurately identify type of SEND in children of colour, but also had much higher expectations about their capabilities (Fox, 2015).
- The non-ideal child is perpetuated and sustained through "teacher bias" (unconscious, conscious, overt and covert) and their everyday actions within early childhood and educational spaces.
- The collateral damage of this teacher bias are the families, and parents who become objects of "surveillance," rather than respected co-educators.
- Both studies in SEND, race and ethnicity emphasise that we must reposition children from problems to learners (Heiskanan et al., 2019; DfE, 2019).

(All taken from Graham et al., 2019)

Supporting the core needs of children with SEND

ACTIVITY

How confident are you in supporting SEND currently?

Very Confident	Confident	Unsure	Not Confident	Not at all Confident
1	2	3	4	5

As we can see, wellbeing is not a straightforward concept. When we begin to think about the different intersections at play, it is vital to develop a tuned-in understanding of our children and their unique needs. One of my frustrations as a SEND specialist is that most tools and documents are designed with the neurotypical child in mind. So, when it comes to children whose needs may expand beyond what we consider "normal," it can be harder to meet those needs and we can therefore feel less confident. Educators should ensure that discussions always include children with SEND and what adjustments might be needed to ensure their full participation.

Deficit lens

Supporting children with SEND can have many ups and downs; in particular, it is not uncommon for families and settings to feel as though they are preparing for the "battlefield" when securing early intervention. Within the early years, a child's SEND is usually identified because of concerns and delays. As educators, we are trained to recognise when development is not taking the usual age and stage related expectations. While this is crucial for early intervention, it also means that we focus predominantly on what the child cannot yet do to ensure that we can put the right support in place. An early years SENCO explains:

EDUCATOR'S VOICE

My focus as a SENCO is ensuring that a child gets what they need. This means that I usually have to communicate to others what a child is like on their "worst day" so that I can prove that they need early support. The habit of describing a child this way can sometimes feel quite harmful because it cultivates this idea that children with SEND are problems to be fixed.

I am, therefore, acutely aware that we must spend our days balancing out those worst days by providing the child with as many good days as possible. I also want to be providing children with a positive sense of self. Our voice becomes their internal voice, so we prioritise cultivating an asset lens, as opposed to a deficit one.

This SENCO could interrogate some of the harmful patterns that emerge out of SEND support through reflective practice. He recognised that he had to actively encourage his team to think about how their words, actions and behaviours can feed into the development of the child's beliefs about themselves. This SENCO provided some parting advice because he noticed that many discussions regarding delays happened in front of children; he reminded his colleagues: *"always speak as though the child you care for can hear you."*

Conclusion

Wellbeing is a heavily featured topic of contemporary early childhood, and despite increased discussions about how this impacts children with SEND, there seem to be fewer supports for equipping educators with the knowledge to succeed. In her book on empathy in the early years, Helen Garnett (2017) informs us that for children to flourish, they need emotional and empathetic "toolkits" that empower and support them to develop lifelong mentally healthy habits. For this to occur, educators need "toolkits" of their own, and there is a definite need for more training beyond universal approaches. As a sector, we must continue to prioritise the right to wellbeing and well-doing for all children, leading to more equitable and inclusive processes.

 Read, watch and listen

Research report
The Flourish model – The Ecology of Wellbeing (2018–2020)
https://www.flourishproject.net/uploads/1/8/4/9/1849450/under-standing_the_flourish_model_july_2018.pdf

Developing a Strengths-Based Approach
https://www.education.vic.gov.au/documents/childhood/profession-als/learning/strengthbappr.pdf

Information Booklet
The Little Book of Flourishing (Wendy Ellyatt, 2018)
Sign up to download: https://www.littlebookofflourishing.com/

Guide to the Equality Act (2010) and Reasonable Adjustments
Council for Disabled Children
https://councilfordisabledchildren.org.uk/sites/default/files/field/atta-
    chemnt/equality-act-early-years_online.pdf

Virtual Continuous Professional (CPD) Development Resource
Harvard Centre for the Developing Child – Executive Function &
    Self-Regulation
https://developingchild.harvard.edu/science/key-concepts/executive
    -function/

Open Access Journal Article
Lundqvist, J., Westling Allodi, M. and Siljehag, E., 2019. Values and
    Needs of Children With and Without Special Educational Needs
    in Early School Years: A Study of Young Children's Views on What
    Matters to Them. *Scandinavian Journal of Educational Research*,
    63(6), pp. 951–967.

Open Access Journal Article
Lewis, A., 2019. Examining the Concept of Wellbeing and Early
    Childhood: Adopting Multi-Disciplinary Perspectives. *Journal of
    Early Childhood Research*, 17(4), pp. 294–308.

Podcast
The Early Years Conversations Podcast
Kate Moxley and Kerry Payne
https://podcasts.apple.com/gb/podcast/early-years-conversations/
    id1514168900

2 | Educator wellbeing in SEND support

STARTING POINTS

In the previous chapter, you began to think about the different ways a child's wellbeing scales could be tipped. Take a few moments to think of the things that might leave you off balance, and reflect on the following:

- How does being off balance make you feel?
- How do the feelings of being unbalanced impact your behaviour and actions?
- Do you have a set of strategies that work for you?

Introduction

It is poignant that in the Early Childhood Educator Wellbeing project, one of the survey respondents stated, "[I] need to be nice no matter how I feel." This highlights an important issue when it comes to wellbeing for the adults who educate and care for young children. According to Kinman, Wray and Strange (2011), the educator role comes with a considerable degree of emotional labour and stress. This is an area of interest for many researchers, leaders and educators, mainly concerning how we manage the emotional consequences of our work. Brackett et al. (2010) found that educators often find themselves engaged in surface acting whereby they hide their true emotional selves and deeply suppress those emotions that might

DOI: 10.4324/9781003138365-2

feel uncomfortable. Doing this over a long time can lead to stress, depression, burnout and compassion fatigue. Even more worryingly, suppressing emotions can contribute to educators "depersonalising" children. During these times, we observe higher levels of adults crowd-controlling children and restricting the diverse ways in which they play and behave. According to Noddings (2013), "If caring is to be maintained, clearly the one caring must be maintained. She must be strong, courageous and capable of joy" (p. 100), but achieving this can be extremely difficult. It can be made more difficult still when the needs of children are broad and not always well understood. In this chapter, we will begin to think about the important influence an educators wellbeing has on children's wellbeing.

RESEARCH SNIPPETS

Research snippets activity

- Research has found that experiences of depression, stress and burnout can reduce how responsive an educator is in practice, and if they face the added challenge of not knowing which strategies to utilise in a moment of psychological distress this can further impact key competencies within their role (Buettner et al., 2016; Hamre and Pianta, 2005; Jennings, 2015).

  Think about the wellbeing scales; what protective factors might prevent this from occurring?

- Poor psychological wellbeing in educators can impact the relationships they build with children and negatively influences the child's social and emotional development (Whitaker et al., 2015; Roberts et al., 2016).

  When discussing children's social and emotional development, do staff consider how they may be influencing behaviour, and the "emotional climate"?

- When educators had more children with behavioural challenges, they spent more time suppressing emotional responses, thus not having time to work through their emotional dysregulation (Frivold and Cameron, 2020).

  In what ways does the setting allow for educators to engage in their own self-regulation?

23

- Teachers of pupils with emotional difficulties have reported wanting opportunities for reflection through objective, solution-focused focused support (Rae, Cowell and Field, 2017).

  Do you take time to decompress when a child has experienced emotional difficulties? How do previous experiences inform future practices?

- Within the context of EY settings, Elfer (2012) proposes that educators involved in interactions that enhance social-emotional learning should be given the opportunity to talk through the emotional demands of their work in a supportive capacity.

  Due to the intense workload in the early years, in what ways might you find opportunities to talk through the emotional demands?

Compassion fatigue – "painting on a smile"

According to NAEYC (2020),

> as an educator, your focus is first and foremost on the children you teach. You also work with family members to support children's learning goals. You carve out time as needed to work with specialists who support the children, team up with colleagues, meet with supervisors, and interact with members of the community. You devote a lot of time, energy and professional responsibilities to many other people, but you may not devote enough time to yourself.
>
> (para. 1)

This constant focus on everything else coming first can lead to stress and compassion fatigue. Compassion fatigue occurs when an educator is overwhelmed or experiences prolonged stress and is unable to prioritise meaningful acts of self-care (Nicholson et al., 2020). They may experience the following symptoms:

- Feeling like nothing is ever good enough.
- Loss of hope and feeling helpless.

- Tiredness.
- Irritability.
- Lack of self-efficacy.
- Anger.
- Fear.
- Losing compassion and the ability to care (empathise).

It is important to understand that compassion fatigue does not mean you do not care, but it impedes your ability to keep pouring from your own emotional cup. Your reserves are empty. There are several ways to address compassion fatigue but at the core of the experience is the need to adjust the expectations we have of ourselves. You might consider the following responses to the experience of compassion fatigue:

- Better out than in ...the most crucial action is to talk to someone to let them know how you are feeling.
- Name it to tame it ... there is an insistence in the early years to hide our uncomfortable emotions but find a safe space or person to explore those feelings and figure out what they mean.
- Utilise the self-care and wellbeing strategies that work for you and double the dosage.
- Speak with your manager to establish what support is available. If they don't know, request that they find out.
- Affirm lived experiences and social identity...it is important to recognise that educators will have positions of power of privilege based on their identity, and this can influence their wellbeing. Promote a culture of listening and validation where there will be a complex dynamic for staff who experience racism, ableism, ageism, sexism and classism.

  Research tells us that when an educator can engage more deeply with their complex emotions, they have lower levels of exhaustion and burnout (Pisaniello, Winefield and Delfabbro 2012). Intriguingly the social and emotional worlds of educators supporting children with SEND is still under-researched.

EDUCATOR'S VOICE

I am an early years SENCO and some days I feel like I am painting on a smile. There is so much of my role where I have to pretend to be someone else, and I couldn't keep it up. We spend so much time teaching children to be who they are, but I couldn't accept my feelings of resentment for my role, the children, my colleagues and the families I worked with. When I decided to stop brushing my feelings under the carpet, I realised that it is normal for our work with children to be challenging and at times adversarial. I remember the first time I sat with a key person and shared my uncomfortable feelings about a child and the tension just lifted immediately. Were we still going to do everything we could to meet this child's needs? Absolutely, but by sharing our fears and vulnerabilities, we ended up working better together. We weren't hiding behind painted smiles. We put together a self-care management plan and though we knew things wouldn't always go to plan, we were better able to accommodate our social and emotional needs, and find solutions rather than more problems.

How comfortable are you with discussing your feelings about your work with children?

Do you have opportunities to explore complex feelings about children's needs?

Burnout in SEND support

Brunsting, Sreckovic and Lane (2014) have found that there are several contributing factors that lead to burnout in SEND support.

Level of experience

It appears, probably unsurprisingly, that the less experience an educator has, the more likely they are to suffer from burnout. In SEND support, it is not uncommon for educators to express their frustration at not fully understanding a child's needs or not having completed training in areas of inclusion that could equip them more fully for the role. The reality is that for many early years educators, their first experience of different types of SEND is when they actually meet the children, which means they are simultaneously required to learn everything they can about the child and their needs while maintaining high-quality education and care. These unrealistic expectations over a long period can result in burnout. One way to mitigate this is to plan specifically for SEND-based training. There can be a tendency to think that completing a SENCO course is sufficient but educators must develop as whole teams. One setting I worked with had a monthly focus and each educator was asked to do some independent research and then they would do a information sharing and strategy workshop. This format helps educators to take initiative and share different perspectives. Another setting invited people in with the lived experience of diability and neurodivergence, and were able to listen to first person perspectives.

Type of disability

The type of disability can contribute to burnout because educators are continuously shifting gears and managing job demands, and if the development needs become more complex or require higher degrees of support, educators may find themselves experiencing stress and exhaustion. It is essential to be clear that this is not the fault of the child but speaks to a broader issue that caregiving roles are generally not well regarded and therefore not always best supported. When a child has a disability or specific care needs, it is important for the setting to complete a care plan so that they can establish what is within their expertise, and where they may need supports. By knowing potential barriers early on, settings can identify if there are any services that can offer their expertise.

Role conflict

It will be unsurprising to many educators that the role of supporting a child with SEND is laden with experiences of conflict. This can occur in many different ways, such as between colleagues, with a parent or specialists. Unfortunately, the SEND support system is often described as a "battlefield" and educators do not escape from this. It is particularly challenging that we are even less supported within the early years, and where a child has emerging needs accessing support can become very difficult. We are often faced with long waiting lists and periods without support, so our time is usually spent battling for that support, which eventually leads to exhaustion.

Role ambiguity

The early years educator role is multi-dimensional and rarely consists of just caring for children. Educators will often feel quite confused about what is expected of them, and the lines become blurred between educators stretching themselves too thinly to meet all the demands of the job or generally withdrawing as much from tasks that they feel are too much. Educators have often shared with me that they resent the volume of work expected from them, especially because they continue to be ill-equipped. Roles and responsibilities should be clear, and where SEND emerges, there should be a sit down discussion to make sure everyone knows what is expected. This also gives everyone the opportunity to address any anxieties and worries.

Lack of administrative support

I recently heard a highly experienced SENCO comment that "SEND = tonnes of paperwork, and that is something we have to accept as part of the job." I disagree entirely with this statement, and it is an area of SEND support that we need to become better at pushing back on. Much of the paperwork or "evidence" we need to gather and prepare leads to the role becoming dominated by procedures rather than spending time with actual children. The high degree of administrative work also leads to burnout. Another SENCO shared with me that he spent more time doing paperwork than supporting educators to provide good early intervention and that his exhaustion resulted from the role becoming completely joyless.

⚖ BURNOUT PROTECTIVE FACTORS

It is important that we take educators' mental health and wellbeing seriously and do not fall into the trap of thinking that basic self-care can resolve some of the more significant emotional and ongoing experiences. In the same way that we develop a wellbeing pedagogy for our children, we must also consider a culture of wellbeing for the whole setting. This can take time and requires a good understanding of the underpinning features of wellbeing. A study by Cigala,

Venturelli and Bassetti (2019) found that there were three dimensions of educator wellbeing which will be addressed below;

A sense of belonging

According to numerous researchers, belonging refers to the perception of being part of a community or group. When we are within our early years spaces, we should feel a sense of belonging, especially as we often spend most of our day within that space. Belonging is cultivated by an educator having a precise role within that group, and so a sense of purpose can be achieved. I always remind educators of the first time they started working in a setting, and how they may have felt out of place or not been quite sure what to do. While those experiences are normal and expected, we might think back to the sense of relief we felt when finally settled into the role, and knew our purpose. Over time, an educator should not need to be told what to do because they belong and understand that space. It is important for leaders and managers to check-in on this sense of belonging, and to identify when an educator might be struggling or lacks a sense of purpose.

A good level of self-efficacy

Self-efficacy is something that we all have and relates to the degree to which we believe we are capable of performing our role well and achieving the goals we set out to do. Self-efficacy links to personal satisfaction and is important in helping us to maintain our ability to carry out our role. Think of the educator who does not think they do their job very well, or who is consistently told that they are underperforming. This has a direct impact on self-efficacy and actually leads to a poorer role performance. That doesn't mean to say that we should not provide constructive feedback but to provide educators with a measured review of their work, and to encourage the act of self-reflection that does not focus purely on the areas of development or weaknesses.

Sawyer et al. (2020) found teachers rated themselves as less efficacious with children with disabilities than children without disabilities. One of the biggest concerns is educators not necessarily knowing how to engage children with SEN and disabilities. Schaefer et al. (2004) stated that this is because disabled children appear to show fewer learning behaviours. An important argument against this viewpoint is that educators are less prepared to understand the diversity of learning behaviours because of the inequitable access to training opportunities for SEND. Interestingly, research has found that educator self-efficacy does increase the more time spent with a disabled child, and this could be the result of forming a connection and developing a deeper understanding of their unique development. The key message is that it can feel daunting when we first realise a child has SEND, and we may be reluctant to lead on support, but taking time to truly get to know a child, and a knowledge of the child's need is vital for both adult and child to thrive.

Agency

A sense of agency is crucial to our wellbeing because as humans, we naturally seek to feel in control of our lives and to be able to have some influence on the situations around us. Agency is the perception of being able to autonomously make decisions and act upon them. Agency has been found to be beneficial for educators and contributes towards them taking an active role within their setting. For example, does the setting SENCO involve the key person in important discussions so that decision making can be collaborative or are they simply told what they should be doing.

When we think of key people involved in SEND support, it is important to consider how we cultivate these dimensions of wellbeing because they will lead to more cohesive whole team approaches. Time invested in staff wellbeing has a knock-on impact on the experiences of children, and so is time never wasted.

Becoming a reflective educator

To do well at work, we must feel well, and the way to monitor this to develop the daily habit of reflection. Think about how often you check-in with yourself or become responsive to different feelings. While reflective practice is talked about a lot in the early years, it can often fall down the list of priorities because it doesn't always feel like it is for the benefit of the person reflecting, rather it becomes an accountability or self-evaluation measure. Time can also factor in when faced with the bustling reality of caring for and educating young children. An educator shared the following reflection:

EDUCATOR'S VOICE

I rarely have time to go to the toilet or think when it gets hectic, and when I hear of reflective practice, I often think that the chance would be a fine thing. Much of my practice involves ticking boxes so that I can actually get on with the job of looking after the kids. I get rather anxious when asked to reflect because it usually translates to agreeing to take on more work or adding to the list of the many ways I can improve.

Limited time was not an uncommon theme when I discussed the practice of reflection with educators, and some also felt that their leaders would often also see it as a form of performance management, thus reducing their motivation further. An educator shared with me that they had lost all motivation to engage in reflective practice when their manager stated, "We just need to get it done in case OFSTED asks us about it."

Reflective practice should serve at least two purposes:

1. To enable an educator to understand their unique practice, pedagogy , personal and professional development.
2. To support the development of inclusive high-quality practice, thus impacting positively on children's and families experiences.

The moment reflection becomes about a regulatory organisation or becomes a tick-box exercise, its purpose becomes null and void because not much is likely to change. Educators should become motivated by reflective practice because they see their growth and learning and how these impact on the children they care for.

When working with a setting on reflection, we developed the "reflecting in the right direction" approach so that educators became driven to focus and celebrate their growth:

The feedback loop accepts you in your totality and works towards your strengths.

Strengths → Areas of development → Weaknesses → Collaboration responsible delegation normalising growth

IDEAS FOR REFLECTING FORWARD

Strengths

It is crucial that a setting works towards each educator's set of strengths. People often live up to their labels, and so we should use positive reinforcement to strengthen practice further. Think about how often the team talks about what each other does well compared to how often they criticise each other's skillsets. Be mindful that strengths are interpreted in different ways but we should allow individuals to embody their self-reported strengths. Challenge the existence of bias.

- Have a feedback book where educators can write about each other's strengths. Share this at team meetings.
- Talk openly about strengths and encourage each other to be proud of the strengths.
- Accept feedback about strengths and avoid rejecting the feedback or balancing it out with a negative.

Areas of development

Every educator will have areas where they will want to develop, and we should encourage a team that can acknowledge where they may have gaps. How well-facilitated are educators to access professional development opportunities, and how creative is the team in helping each other out to grow?

- Plan realistic and manageable actions to address your areas of development.
- Ask for support from a trusted colleague.
- Complete "bitesize" CPD to gradually develop your knowledge.
- Acknowledge that failure is on the pathway to success. What did you learn, and what will you do next time?

Weakness

Some educators and leaders will shy away from using the term "weakness," but we have to accept that not every educator can be good at everything. And in some cases, they have a specific weakness. Educators need to be in the presence of colleagues who accept that some weaknesses aren't necessarily going to be overcome.

Also be mindful here that you may have disabled or neurodivergent educators who have identified specific limitations relating to their condition … it is here that you will need to make reasonable adjustments.

- Be open to those things you struggle with or feel are weaknesses.
- If someone highlights a weakness, and you disagree, be open to having a discussion about your interpretations.
- Gain feedback about the reasonable steps you can take to address the weaknesses.
- Ask about what can be negotiated to ensure you can still work within your limitations.

"Good enough" approach

The setting should adopt a "good enough" approach to educator skill sets. The job is complex and requires lots of key skills. Our aim should be to support them to be good enough because perfect is impossible.

- Ensure that educators feel that there is a culture of "I am by your side-ness" rather than one in which they have a fear of the repercussions of failure.
- Use collaboration so that each other's skillsets can bounce off each other.
- Delegate responsibly, rather than to test someone's capacity.
- Normalise growth, and allow educators to learn, unlearn, re-learn and change their minds about things.

HOW TO REFLECT WHEN YOU ARE BUSY

The practice of bitesize reflections can be beneficial for building habits when you are busy. Consider the following tasks:

- At the end of each day, use your phone to either note or voice record one thing that went well, one thing that challenged you, and a possible solution. Over a month, you will notice that you are building up lots of reflections and the intent to reflect should transfer to your everyday actions.

- Set up a staff mood check-in so each morning, staff either put a feelings card into a box and then the manager can use this to sense the mood climate for the day. If, for example, lots of educators have dropped in an unhappy emotion, it might not be the day for a huge project or team meeting after work.
- A tweet a day – set up a Twitter account for your eyes only and write out a reflection a day. It only allows a certain number of characters, and you can scroll back through and search for patterns and trends in your reflections.
- Set up a Google Drive document and ask educators to contribute their reflections across the month. As a team, you can then visually see thinking in action, in the moment and over time.
- Use a Mentimetre regularly asking educators to submit key words about how they are thinking and feeling. Compare it over time to establish the emotional climate of the setting.

INDIVIDUAL AND GROUP SUPERVISION

When we think of supervision, we might think of it as a process for monitoring staff performance, but within early education, it provides a real opportunity for mentoring and coaching so that we can grow and evolve. According to Gasper and Walker (2020), supervision should be relationship-based and have person-centred roots. It is not the space in which educators should be appraised. Supervision should contribute towards an educators wellbeing because it is a process in which they have a safe space to reflect upon their role. Many settings find supervision quite difficult because it is a time-consuming process, and the mentor is rarely has access to specific and ongoing training to complete the role. So, while supervision is a statutory and expected practice, there are also many ways in which it does not function in the way it should. I spoke to several educators and leaders about supervision to try and gain an insight into how it practically works, and this led to some interesting discussions, as outlined below.

Walk and talk supervisions

EDUCATOR'S VOICE

I had read an article by the Early Childhood Educator Wellbeing group that said that although educators never physically stop, it is more that we spend a lot of our time lifting children, or getting down to their level, and that actually, we do not always get our step counts in. This really stuck with me as a manager because I know that walking is a perfect way to clear my head and to think straight. I will be honest, I really don't like supervision, because no matter how much I try to make it supportive, I am still sitting across from someone as their leader trying to play the role of a therapist. It doesn't always feel genuine or comfortable, and so I introduced walk and talk supervisions. Even if it is just around the block a few times, I get my staff moving. It has made such a difference. Suddenly all that formality drops and we talk more openly about what is going on. Obviously, there are ground rules for talking about work while walking and not sharing confidential information, and I conduct safeguarding supervisions more formally, but this has my staff enjoying a time out from the setting and an opportunity to talk about what's on their mind.

Using a supervision framework

Supervision discussions are difficult with less experienced members of staff and I was always just getting, "everything is fine." I developed a supervision framework which tackled different aspects of practice, including one for SEND support. The idea is that educators have a copy of the framework, and they make notes around it across a four-week period, and we then use this to guide our discussions. I am trying to help my key people become more accountable when leading on SEND support, and when we discuss individual children, the framework enables a deeper discussion about the quality of that support.

ACTIVITY

As a team, each talk about the positive feelings you experience being an educator. Discuss what experiences provide you with a sense of purpose and describe your best day at work. Discuss how achievable those feelings and experiences are and agree whether these are an individual or collective set of responsibilities.

- Agree on daily wellbeing habits.
- Make a list of "pressed buttons" so that each educator is aware of the things that negatively impact wellbeing and take intentional steps to avoid pressing them.

- Build the "favoured feelings" into your everyday vocabulary so that you can reinforce the positive aspects of the educator role. Remember that feelings often invoke memories, or we associate them with events and experiences, and it might be that we are encouraged to do more of what makes us feel good when we are working.

Wellbeing strategies

Action learning sets for wellbeing

One of the most significant activities for developing my wellbeing practice was taking part in action learning sets. When we are in a challenging situation, it can be tough to think straight or be solution-focused, and we must reach out and ask for help in these moments. As the saying goes, a problem shared is a problem halved, and it can be a compelling learning experience when working with young children who we have not yet connected with or we are having difficulty coming to understand. The premise of an action learning set is that you present your challenge to a group of others, and they work it out for you. It is very much about capacity building, and below is a guide of how to do it:

1. Spend 5–10 minutes discussing the problem you are facing.
2. Spend 5–10 minutes receiving "quickfire" questions from the group to understand the situation.
3. The group then spends 10–15 minutes discussing the problem coming up with ideas, suggestions and advice. At this point, you remain completely quiet, which can be hard, and you can take notes or reflect on the points being made.
4. Spend 5 minutes providing feedback and agree on which actions you will take forward.

Gathering others' perspectives who may see the situation more clearly or differently can help an educator work through a problem without feelings of isolation and being deskilled.

Creating a wellbeing blueprint

"Our feelings are our most genuine paths to knowledge."
—Audre Lorde

Each educator will have their own idea about what wellbeing means to them individually. A really good activity to do as a team is to complete your own wellbeing blueprints. Have a file within the setting so that you each know how to support each other with wellbeing. Try the following ...

Create a table with two columns, in one have:

"My wellbeing priorities"

There are days when things may feel too much, and your wellbeing may feel impacted. When stressed, it can be difficult to focus on the small steps to feeling well. Use the column to outline your main wellbeing priorities and ensure that you make time for small pleasures. These things might not solve all your problems, but small acts of self-care can be nourishing

"How *you* can support my wellness"

Your wellbeing blueprint is unique to you, and on those days when you do not feel your best, it can make a world of difference if someone supports your wellness. Create a list of five things that help with your wellness and share it with colleagues. When stressed or anxious, we can forget to turn to the things that we know will help. Having colleagues who know your five ways back to thriving mean that you can support each other.

Codeword

When you are on the ground working every day in a busy environment, it can be difficult to indicate that you may be struggling, need support or need to leave the environment for the sake of your wellbeing. The use of an agreed codeword can be helpful so that your colleagues know when you have reached a point in which you need help. This also reduces the occurrence of educators engaging in conversations that might not be appropriate in tone in front of children. The codeword indicates a call for help without an educator having to justify their reasons because often when stressed, it can be much harder to articulate what is happening. It is an agreed word between colleagues that helps to avoid the escalation of stress.

Strategies to avoid

"Leave your baggage at the door" mentality

One of the most common strategies we hear of in early years environments is to "leave your baggage at the door," which essentially means to place your experiences and emotions aside so that the main task at hand can be done. Although educators need to be very mindful and aware of boundaries, it is important to acknowledge that separating yourself from your experiences and emotions can be harmful. Educators should have spaces to store that emotional baggage within the setting so that they can do their jobs. One of my previous managers, would always say "drop your baggage in here and I will look after it for you." It was such a subtle comment, but conveyed that sometimes we just need someone to hold in mind that we are managing both our personal and professional selves.

EDUCATOR'S VOICE

One of my staff could become quite volatile when she was stressed. It was affecting her relationship with her colleagues, and they sometimes described her as a "ticking time bomb." I asked her how what she usually did when she was flipping her lid. She explained that at home, she would get up and move or exercise because she felt like she was full of anger, and it always helped to release pent up adrenaline. I advised that where possible she let me know when she got to that point, and I would accommodate her being able to talk a walk around the block. Over time, more staff started utilising the "around the block strategy." We ended up talking about the idea that childcare requires movement, but it isn't always the best for regulating emotions because it is usually heavy lifting, standing and domestic work. I recommended she find a way to actually do exercise during the day, and she started bringing her running gear to work. She would do a 20-minute run at lunch, and the difference it made to her mood was astonishing (not every day, mind). It spurred lots of us to find ways to exercise during the day. Eventually, I invested in an exercise bike for the staff room and some weights. Literally, when we are stressed, we will go and do ten mins on the bike, and it is even great when having conversations/mini meetings. One of my staff calls it the "idea bike." My main aim was to provide an outlet for that rush of adrenaline we feel when we are angry.

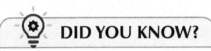

DID YOU KNOW?

Stress is contagious

Have you ever been in a situation where you have entered an early childhood environment and sensed an atmosphere or tension? When speaking with an educator, they explained that they worked in a baby room with a team of unhappy staff who often felt stressed. They would often blame the children's moods, but they had not considered that it was their own states of mind and stress that was contributing to that stressful atmosphere.

Studies have found evidence that stress is contagious. According to Carnevali et al. (2017), the stress levels of another person can trigger a physiological and behavioural response in others. This includes both during and in the aftermath of stress (Waters, West and Mendes, 2014). It is, therefore, important to acknowledge when we are stressed, particularly when we are around other caregivers and children. One of the best responses to a stressful environment is to utilise some of the strategies that we use with children. The following case study demonstrates a response to stress using movement:

Intersectionality and wellbeing of staff

When we think of young children, we consider all the different factors that may impact their access to the feelings of wellbeing, but it is important to remember that as adults, there are also lots of different factors that might influence our wellbeing as well. I am, for example, a neurodivergent educator with a diagnosis of attention deficit hyperactivity disorder (ADHD), and despite experiencing many positive traits, I also face lots of limitations as well. I noticed that when I was in a busy space for long periods of time, I would often feel overloaded by sensory triggers and so I had to recognise that my wellbeing was impacted by long periods of time spent in one space. My manager offered for me to take "brain breaks" during the day and asked me to provide a list of suitable mini breaks which would then support my ongoing attention and self-regulation. Other staff had other needs, and they were also accommodated. This idea of staff needing different things to thrive helped us to understand equity for staff, but also equity for children. We are not one size fits all, we can fit differently into our educator roles.

Conclusion

As educators, we must become skilled at balancing our personal and professional identities to provide adequate caregiving and education. Children depend so heavily on a network of secure and consistent relationships that this can require high degrees of emotional labour from the educator. The complexity of caregiving is often overlooked, misunderstood or belittled, and many people can take a reductionist view of the work involved in caring for and educating young children. Additionally, children are not a homogenous group, and each child comes with their unique learning behaviours, characteristics and needs. In most cases, early years educators are trained to support typically developing children but are also expected to meet a wide range of developmental needs, differences and delays. They must also be aware of the contextual factors that may confound some of a child's learning challenges and be equipped to engage in early intervention tasks. The expectations just continue to pile up, leaving educators vulnerable to stress, depression, burnout, and compassion fatigue.

The ways forward with this issue require much greater efforts from our government to invest in and recognise the value of well-supported educators, but we must turn to each other while we advocate for this to change. An educator's best resource is usually a colleague or network of others who understand the unique challenges. Nawana Parker (2020) makes a significant point about wellbeing, stating that we often fall into the cultural trap of putting our settings, children and families first "no matter what" because it comes with the territory of being an early year's educator. But while you are using every resource to support others, you are eventually running out of battery for yourself. I often think of computer game characters who have to recharge their batteries, and I realise that educators will often carry on even when there is a red flashing light telling them to stop or it will be "game over." It is important that as an educator you understand your boundaries for caregiving and learn to speak up or say no to things that are beyond your emotional capacity. This can feel daunting and defiant, but if it is for the purpose of reserving energy to be better at the role, it is a worthy boundary to have.

Read, watch and listen

Kate Moxley
Wellness for All
https://katemoxleyeyc.co.uk/wellbeing/

SEND Supervision Framework
www.eyfs4me.com

Wellbeing Blueprint
www.eyfs4me.com

Preventing Compassion Fatigue – Caring for Yourself
https://www.naeyc.org/resources/pubs/yc/jul2020/preventing-com-passion-fatigue

Podcast
The Early Years Conversations Podcast
Compassion Fatigue
Kate Moxley and Kerry Payne
https://podcasts.apple.com/gb/podcast/early-years-conversations/
    id1514168900

3 | Social, emotional and/or mental health

Defining social, emotional and mental health difficulties (SEMH)

Children may experience a range of social and emotional difficulties, which will be presented and communicated in different ways. SEMH may be a primary need or the result of other needs. Children will usually communicate their needs through various behaviours, either becoming

DOI: 10.4324/9781003138365-3

withdrawn and isolated, or using distressed behaviours that we might describe as challenging. These behaviours can indicate an underlying unresolved need such as experiencing anxiety, stress or depression. Children with attachment insecurity, attention deficit hyperactivity disorder (ADHD) and autism are likely to experience social, emotional and mental health difficulties. The ability to manage feelings and behaviours for children with SEND may be more difficult, including both the development of self-regulation and executive functions.

Starting points

There has been a significant increase in our understanding of attachment-aware and trauma-informed practice in the early years. We often hear lots of terminology related to social, emotional and/or mental health. Research suggests that much of the "good practice" around attachment and mental health is intuitively learnt rather than accessed through training and qualifications (Page and Elfer, 2013). There are also increasing discussions around problems in applying attaching theory universally, and the ways in which it fails to account for cultural diversity (Stern, Barbarin & Cassidy, 2021). Look at the list below. How would you rate your confidence in the areas listed, and how might you account for cultural variations?

Social, emotional and mental health concepts					
Concept	1	2	3	4	5
	(very confident)	(confident)	(aware but unsure)	(no confident)	(Very unconfident)
Co-regulation					
Attachment theory					
Co-Regulation					
Adverse childhood experiences (ACEs)					
Self-regulation					
Secure base					
Attachment					
Toxic stress					
Early intervention					

ACTIVITY

Now consider the following when reflecting back on how confident you rated yourself:

1. I understand the definition or basic principles of this concept. **(Yes/No)**
2. I have attended training which has provided me with the skills and knowledge to understand this concept, and this has taken into account cross-cultural perspectives? **(Yes/No)**
3. I know how to support these concepts in practice, including teaching, strategies and evidence-based approaches. **(Yes/No)**
4. These concepts were part of my qualifications. **(Yes/No)**
5. I could teach and support others in understanding these concepts. **(Yes/No)**

Reflection

Using this exercise as a starting point is essential because up-to-date knowledge and skills in these areas is crucial if we are to positively influence the social and emotional experiences of young children. If I think back to my own practice, I was not fully introduced to attachment theory until I was six years into my career. In my discussions with other educators, many may have completed "one-off" courses or independently researched these key concepts, but developing a steady foundation of consistent and well informed practice can be difficult and subject to misinterpretation. For example, we often hear the term "self-regulation" as a stand-alone concept, rather than in conjunction with the formative and ongoing experience of co-regulation. It is essential to establish here that this chapter addresses some key concepts but ongoing access to training and skills development is also essential, along with tuning into individual and subjective social and emotional needs. Understanding SEMH is an ongoing and active process and should be underpinned by a commitment to understanding contemporary research and practice, including critiques of pioneers and theories that can lack diversity, equity and cross-cultural perspectives. What is even more important is that despite growing awareness, we do not see a decline in poor mental health; instead, we see a greater need for support and emphasis that systemic inequalities continue contribute to inequitable support. This is particularly pertinent since the start of a global pandemic, and the implications of this on children's wellbeing is still being fully realised.

Introduction

Right relationships

When I heard the quote, "no significant learning can happen without a significant relationship" (Comer, 1995), it immediately made me think of my own attachment story and how feelings of not being safe and secure impacted and impeded my learning. Attachment refers to the enduring bonds that form throughout our early relationship experiences. These experiences provide attachment patterns and influence whether we feel secure or insecure in the world. Not feeling safe can be the ultimate distraction for children, tugging away at their hearts and minds, and usually they find themselves under the additional and mounting pressures of adult expectations. When we are with young children, we must focus on how we can relate to them because we are, after all, former children who have already navigated our way through the ups and downs of childhood. It always amazes me how adults can act so distant from their childhood selves and judge children for the very behaviours and emotions that they likely still exhibit as adults. For example, think about how worry or uncertainty impacts you as an adult and how it weaves into your everyday life. We can usually work our way through this because we have learnt to manage our feelings and behaviours, and it is with this knowledge; we can teach children how to do the same, through a process known as co-regulation. Children need to know that we have been there too and that we are by their side as they grow. We do not necessarily have control of the relationships a child has outside of our setting, and we must be careful not to be judgemental, but we can be decisive in providing the safety and security that they need to learn.

An educational psychologist once said to me, "no child should leave your setting having survived the relationship they had with you; rather, they should be thriving because of it." We must never underestimate the privilege we possess by being an initial part of the fabric of a child's early relationships. Having responsive early experiences from caregivers provides opportunities for a child to build trust in the world around them and further cultivates their creativity and curiosity to continue to make a more comprehensive network of connections from adults to peers. There are many reasons why a child might not create those social networks early on, such as non-responsive caregiving, adverse childhood experiences (ACEs) or developmental differences, which are not fully understood or supported.

What we do know is that children are born to connect, and in the context of their early relationships, they gradually learn how to interact with the world around them. We must be mindful, however, that our relationships may take more time and patience when a child has SEND because it may take longer to figure each other out due to the differences in development. For example, it may take longer to understand the communication preferences and meanings of a non-speaking child, or developing trust could be harder for a child who has experienced trauma or adversity.

Howes (2000 p. 257) explains that we are creating an "emotional climate" through relationships, practice and provision. Before we begin to think about social, emotional and mental health, consider how the "emotional climate" can tip the wellbeing scales. What relational practices and strategies could help or hinder?

Social, emotional and mental health

Social	Emotional	Mental health
Early social and emotional development is defined as the emerging capacity of young children to "form close and secure adult and peer relationships; experience, regulate and express emotions in socially and culturally appropriate ways; and explore the environment and learn – all in the context of family, community, and culture" (Yates et al., 2008).		Mental health encompasses the full continuum of health promotion, prevention, mental illness and intervention that addresses children's social and emotional health (Zeanah, Stafford, Nagle and Rice, 2005). Infants and very young children naturally experience stress, and it is both the caregiving relationship and environment that can shape physical, cognitive development, and emotional development (Shonkoff, Lippitt and Cavanaugh, 2000). Mental health is something we all possess and not the absence of mental illness.

It is essential to understand that everyone has mental health, and they will experience optimal and adverse periods of health and illness dependent on different biological, genetic and environmental factors. It is a term often immediately confused with mental illness, but it is more nuanced than this, and while some people may go on to experience mental illness educators need to be aware of the differences and subtleties in language. This is particularly important in the early years sector as there has been an increase in diagnosable mental health conditions such as anxiety disorders.

NHS Digital has found that one in six children aged between 5 and 16 years has a mental health condition (2020), and in light of the COVID-19 pandemic there has been an increase in abuse rates, which will undoubtedly have an impact on wellbeing. Alarmingly, NHS Digital also found that 1 in 18 children aged between 2 to 4 years had a diagnosable mental health condition, and the data suggested that boys were more impacted than girls (2017), although we must consider the underrepresentation of gender in special needs data sets. The findings also indicated that children with other diagnosable conditions such as Autism and behaviour "disorders" were at greater risk of mental health conditions. On an international level, mental health problems in childhood are considered a global public health issue, affecting up to 20% of children (Bayer et al., 2008). And so, what we need to consider as educators is how we can place social, emotional and mental health at the centre of our practice as a priority and ensure that support is adapted to meet the broad range of needs those children present with. If we know that relationships are the key to wellbeing, it is important to begin with the fundamental concepts of attachment.

Attachment theory, wellbeing and SEND

 **RESEARCH SNIPPETS**

The ingredients of an attachment-informed setting

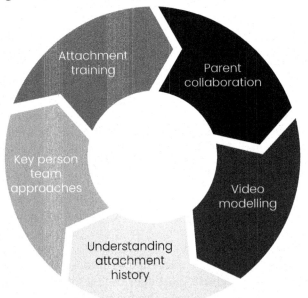

- A study found that educators' understanding of attachment-informed practices was mainly developed through intuition instead of professional development training and qualifications

(Page and Elfer, 2013). The same study found that this created anxiety for educators unsure of how to best navigate the emotional complexity of relationships in a professional caregiving role.

- Research suggests that early years educators' development of attachment awareness practice is best supported through emotional education and professional development opportunities, and that a focus on emotional development significantly increases the quality of care over time. In addition, educators do not require extensive training, rather short but regular bursts (Biringen et al., 2012; Shonkoff and Phillips, 2002).

- Attachment training that demonstrates how theory translates to practice enhances opportunities for children to develop secure attachments, and educators have been found to show greater sensitivity when more fully informed of children's needs.

- Attachment awareness does not only improve the relationships between adults and children but leads to educators increased motivations and positive attitudes towards their careers (Aylward and O'Neill, 2009; Ebbeck et al., 2015).

- Research has found that team activities such as video interventions helps caregivers to increase their self-reflection and self-awareness, which is the first step to behavioural change.

- Regular access to CPD around attachment-based topics leads to educators being more positive about and towards children. Hence, children benefit significantly from childcare settings in which professional development and special training are a regular practice.

- Holistic attachment awareness, which includes the parents, generated highly positive outcomes for child–parent relationships and secure attachment and can serve as a model for programmes aimed to increase parental sensitivity. It is also important to listen to parents perspectives when thinking about attachment, and different family customs, cultures and beliefs. Attachment theory should not be universally applied as this can lead to bias, or believing that one size fits all. Attachment practices look different across cultures.

- A 2013 US-based study entitled "The Missing Piece" asked educators what they thought could fix the problem of static educational achievements (Bridgeland et al., 2013). Results indicated that teachers overwhelmingly agreed that social and emotional learning is the missing piece to boost outcomes and transform our schools.

In what ways do you prioritise attachment awareness? Consider the following:

- Having a specific training plan for attachment-aware professional development.
- Offer bitesize opportunities to learn about attachment.
- Request specific training from local services such as the local authority.

Attachment-informed key people

The power of caregiving

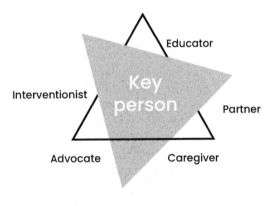

The key person is a relationship-based system that should be attachment-informed. Educators should have a good grasp of the ways to support safety, security and flourishing. Working in the early years is often a complex task of juggling many priorities, but none of this should be at the expense of building connections with children. This circle of security is the space from which children learn to explore, take risks, play and learn.

In his book, *The Body Keeps the Score*, Bessel Van Der Kolk (2014) explains the journey of attachment and says

as we grow up, we gradually learn to take care of ourselves both physically and emotionally, but we get our first lessons in self-care from the way that we are cared for. Mastering the skill of self-regulation depends to a large degree on how harmonious our early interactions with our caregivers are.

(p. 111)

It is rather peculiar that this fundamental act and the power of caregiving is so often looked down upon. The image above positions the key person as fulfilling an essential role in attachment development. An educator once described to me how she sees herself as the "back up system," and this idea of becoming a buffer to secure attachment is significant when we think about the diverse experiences of the children we care for. Children with SEND need dependent and consistent relationships for a wide range of reasons, and the following is an outline of key practices that every key person should adopt to support essential attachment practices.

Secure base

According to Bowlby (1988), children need to be in the context of a secure base in their earliest years, and through their connections with a caregiver, the child begins to feel safe enough that they can go on to explore the world around them. It is quite interesting to observe a child who will explore and frequently return to re-establish feelings of safety in the presence of a secure base. I once heard this described as introducing the world to the child in "small doses," and through this back-and-forth process, children develop an "in-sync" relationship with people and the environment. While children should be in the presence of a secure base, it is not uncommon for children to receive inconsistent caregiving. This can occur from both a parenting perspective but also from the key person. For example, high staff turnover can lead to changes in key people, or experiencing lots of transitions where the child is cared for by multiple people and inconsistencies build in responsive caregiving.

This can become particularly challenging if a child has SEND and where the development is not yet fully understood. A key observation I made when supporting early years settings is that educators can experience quite complex emotions when supporting a child that does not fit into their ideas of a "normal child," and this lack of understanding can cause feelings of isolation and feeling deskilled. When attempts to soothe, distract or resolve are unsuccessful, the educator can feel an acute sense of failure. If this continues without support, the educator may give up trying, become resentful or be generally inconsistent. This situation leads to a child whose needs are not being met. If we think of how we form adult relationships, we will likely describe them as being quite different from one to the other; for example, we might categorise our friendships differently based on the qualities or traits of the individual. We are generally quite flexible that attachment patterns vary between adults; in other words, we learn to adapt. It is important to remember that attachments come in all shapes and sizes, and connections can take time.

The dance of attunement

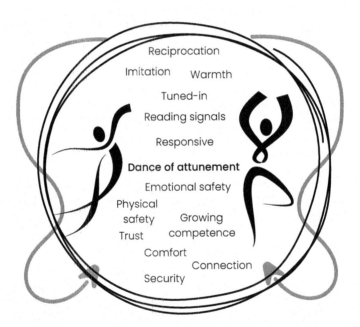

According to Van Der Kolk (2014), secure attachment happens when there is a process of emotional attunement. At the most basic level, children seek to have their needs met, so through subtle tuning-in the adult reads the signals of the child and responds to them. For a baby, this might be how a parent can distinguish between different types of crying, and the parent will know whether the child is hungry, sleepy or just in need of a snuggle. As children grow, they look for signs of connection with their caregivers as confirmation that they are being understood. This is a cognitive process, and researchers have identified mirror neurons that begin functioning in infancy and are activated when the child picks up the imitations and emotional states of an attachment figure. The adult and child's interactions sync up both emotionally and physically (Tronick, 2003), and so the emotional regulation of the adult is felt by the child. When the child has positive associations of safety, comfort and knowing their needs will be met, they become more tolerant of higher arousal levels (stress). This does not imply that adults must be in a constant state of calm; rather, they can maintain their balance when stressed and find ways back to states of relaxation. If we think back to the wellbeing scales and imagine that both child and adult are in the process of striking this equilibrium. To use another analogy, as an adult and child begin to connect and understand each other, they are engaged in a dance of attunement. This idea of a dance is essential, especially when we think of children with SEND and whose need for consistency may be higher but harder to achieve. I discussed this idea with a key person and SENCO, who explained the following:

EDUCATOR'S VOICE

I love the idea of the dance of attunement, and on paper it probably seems quite straightforward. A child has a need or arousal, and as adults we identify that need and help a child find their way back to relaxation, but I often find that we are all doing different styles of dancing and to different music. So, the dance of attunement can actually be quite chaotic if we haven't found the time to really tune-in and work out the child's signals. The way I see it is that there are lots of different ways to dance and other genres of music, and so we have to think about how those styles of dance can become fused. My point is that this dance of attunement is not a straightforward attachment process, particularly if a child has developmental differences. But that doesn't mean to say that it cannot be achieved. You might need to dance more often or learn some of their moves, and more than anything, we just have embrace the fact that patience and practice will help us to find that rhythm.

Another important aspect of attunement is that the adult aims to provide the child with agency and independence over time. Again, when we think of SEND, there can be a tendency to think of children who cannot do things, who depend more heavily on adult support, and who have little autonomy. It can be easy to fall into the trap of attunement without cultivating and assuming competency along the way. For children with SEND, we may need to offer adaptations or find alternative ways for a child to identify what makes them feel a sense of wellness and autonomy (2015).

NAMING IT TO TAME IT

Reflection

Have you ever been in a situation where you feel an emotion but you can't quite put your finger on it? You may wake up in the morning and not feel quite right, or you may confuse emotions, for example, excitement and anxiety.

Emotions are complicated things, and again this is an area where we expect children to be much more emotionally intelligent than they perhaps are. Even as adults, trying to name and understand feelings and emotions is difficult. Beyond the core emotions of happiness, sadness, anger and shame, there are many more at play in our everyday lives. Finding ways to communicate our emotions is often vital to understanding them, and I always encourage children and adults to be prepared to do a bit of emotional detective work because our feelings can be deceptive. As Alain de Botton states in *Conversations on Love* (Lunn, 2021): "our emotions are not entirely reliable: they tend to overshoot or undershoot the target" (p. 17). Another really important consideration is that neurodivergent children often experience greater difficulties with understanding emotions and feelings. For example, autistic children commonly experience alexithymia, which is defined as difficulties in identifying and distinguishing emotions and bodily sensations (Goerlich, 2018). It is, therefore, important that within our practice, we have robust support and strategies to develop responsive co-regulation strategies.

THE EMOTIONAL CHAMELEON CASE STUDY

The tricky thing about emotions is that they can often disguise themselves as each other. When working in a reception class, an educator supported a child on the diagnosis pathway for ADHD. He observed the child and noticed that he would become very hyperactive and excitable when there were many distractions or noise. He would almost "jump into the chaos." The educator explained that he often thought that the child seemed quite happy when this was happening, but over time he sensed a brimming anxiety as he came to be more attuned to the child's personality. He decided to help channel the child's emotions and actions, and so together they would do some sensory break movements and focus on regulating breathing together. He also began thinking of creative ways to ask how he felt and this really helped the educator to understand the experience of hyperactivity. For example, "Does it feel like you have buzzy bees in your body or like you are on a rollercoaster?" This way, the educator could identify the type of stress response the child may be experiencing.

Co-regulation and self-regulation

Co-regulation refers to the supportive, interactive process between an adult and child when a child is learning to manage, moderate and regulate their emotional experiences (Kostol and Cameron, 2020). The ability and skill of helping to hold and contain a child's emotions are important in the development of later self-regulation, which is the ability to control and influence the emotions they have and how they experience and express them (Gross, 1998). It is crucial to recognise that self-regulation cannot happen without co-regulation and that our expectations for a child to manage their feelings and emotions should be realistic and responsive to the child's individual needs.

In our everyday practices, we have opportunities to help children to prepare for self-regulation, for example, by recognising and identifying children's emotional expressions and then responding to these experiences with guidance, love, patience, understanding and support. Co-regulation comprises a set of supportive and reciprocated interactions between the child and caring adults, often referred to as serve and return interactions. According to Murray et al. (2015), we use our own self-regulation skills to support a child through modelling, coaching and helping a child to learn how to express, understand and resolve emotional experiences. In other words, our ability to self-regulate is critical in supporting the self-regulation of children.

 CASE STUDY

Part 1

I led in the 0–2s room for a year, and an 18-month-old child started at the setting with learning difficulties. The nature of the child's difficulties was still being investigated by the doctors, but the child was mainly non-speaking and had prolonged periods of distress. It was a situation in which I figured I would be okay because I generally felt confident with child development for under 2s. Lots of the children had minimal but developing language, and periods of crying were commonplace. This child, however, could not be settled, and as the room leader I felt myself becoming increasingly panicked that I had no idea how to help resolve the feelings the child was experiencing. I tried every strategy I could think of, and I was in regular communication with both the parents and the specialist services. I was reassured that settling would take time, and I was clearly doing everything within my power to support the child, but I became overpowered by thoughts that I was no good at my job. I dreaded going into work and it made me increasingly uncomfortable that I felt resentment towards the child. When you start working with children, it can be all too easy to have this ideal scenario of a picture-perfect set-up with play, joy and love, but this was just constant stress all day and every day. Admitting that I was spiralling did not feel like an option, but I needed help.

- *Do you relate to this situation or something similar?*
- *What feelings might be invoked when we are trying practices strategies and they don't appear to work?*

- *What might the educator have done in this scenario?*
- *What type of response and support could have been offered by the setting?*

Part 2

I went along to one of my supervision sessions soon thereafter, and it was here that I became very emotional and shared my feelings of isolation and sense of failure. To my surprise, my manager fully embraced the situation and opened up space for me to talk openly and honestly. She shared an example of a similar situation when she was an educator and realised that she could have been better prepared for this. Together we sat and agreed a plan of action and considered a more personalised settling-in period. We had an open discussion with the parents about some of our vulnerabilities when supporting SEND. At the root of my fear was that I wanted a relationship with the child, but I didn't know how to get there, and so I knew we needed to break things down into more manageable steps. I am not saying it was smooth sailing or easy, but I realised that to form an attachment with a child, we also need to be in the context of supportive relationships within our setting. I suffered silently for weeks because I assumed I was failing, but actually it was a child who needed me to persevere in establishing those early connections. Six months later and we are best buddies, and I am now starting to do short visits with him to the toddler room. Neither of us are ready to transition yet, and he needs some more time in the safe haven of my baby room, but I am so glad we could find a way forward together.

This key person used the following co-regulation strategies to support the child:

- Interacting in warm, responsive ways.
- Building knowledge of the child's individual cues and responding consistently. This included asking for ideas from the parents about home routines.

- Providing physical and emotional comfort when a child is distressed.
- Modifying the child's environment to decrease demands and stress, for example, spending time outside.
- Providing consistent routines and structure.
- Modelling self-calming strategies and talking to the child about routines and rhythms.

Quick fixes do not work in co-regulation

When a child is dysregulated or stressed, what is your immediate response? For many educators, the answer to this question is to stop or reduce the source of stress. Research, however, has found that "quick fixes" can actually be unhelpful for children's social and emotional development. According to Kostol and Cameron (2020), opportunities for co-regulation, which lead to growth in children's self-regulatory skills (Gillespie, 2015), may be lost when the emphasis is placed first and foremost on reducing the impact of stressful situations by resolving them too quickly, for example, through distraction.

Given that awareness of one's own emotions is an important aspect of co-regulation, allowing the adult to keep calm and soothe the emotionally distressed child is critical (Guo et al., 2015; Silkenbeumer, Schiller and Kärtner, 2018). Indeed, finding ways to emotionally "meet" the child, or provide affirmation of their emotional state, was also described by several participants as having a calming effect on children. Research indicates that helping children find words or ways to communicate difficult emotions can reduce levels of stress with respect to negative emotional situations (Lieberman et al., 2007). When you do this with children with SEND this may include visuals, physical actions or non-speaking interactions.

It takes two

It is often overlooked that a key person attachment involves two people, the adult and the child, and we must consider that key people are often expected to support attachment-informed relationships with several children at once. That is a lot of containment, and it is crucial that settings have supportive systems in place that strengthen each other's capacity to provide responsive caregiving. Settings should consider the following:

- How key people are supported in their attachments with multiple children, and ways to ensure that the container of emotions does not overflow, for example using a buddy key person system.
- Encouraging vulnerability and an open dialogue about the complexity of attachments, and the emotional and physical toll.
- Holding each other in mind as well as the children, for example, checking in on each other, and being nearby during co-regulation as a backup support.
- Using active listening and seeking to understand as well as being understood.

Adverse childhood experiences and trauma

Adverse childhood experiences (ACEs), along with related terms such as childhood trauma and maltreatment, refer to a range of negative childhood experiences. The World Health Organisation defines childhood trauma and adversity as all forms of physical and emotional abuse, neglect or exploitation that results in actual or potential harm to a child (Butchart et al., 2006). ACEs may include, but are not limited to, physical, sexual and emotional abuse, bullying, parental death or loss, neglect and poverty (Felitti et al., 1998)

Overwhelming evidence for the impact of ACEs on outcomes in adulthood is also apparent within mental health literature, and it has been estimated that in the absence of childhood adversity, there would be a 22.9% reduction in mood difficulties, 31% reduction of anxiety, 41.6% reduction of behavioural difficulties, 27.5% reduction of substance-related difficulties (Kessler et al., 2010) and a 33% reduction in psychosis (Varese et al., 2012). This type of data alone indicates why it is crucial we try to mitigate the risks of adversity early on in life.

Trauma and stress

In her book *The Trauma and Attachment-Aware Classroom*, Rebecca Brooks (2020) provides a good analogy for early healthy development, neuroscience and attachment. She asks, "How much attention do you pay to the foundations of your house?" For many, it is likely something that we don't often consider until something goes wrong, or if we want to do some home improvement. But generally, the structure and architecture of our homes provide safety, and assurance so we can go about our everyday lives. Brooks compares this to the developing brain, in that a strong foundation and repeated positive early experiences communicate safety and security and means that children can explore and learn in a relatively stress-free state. Not all children, however, have these strong foundations, and this could be due to a range of genetic, biological and environmental reasons. Without these foundations, it can make it very hard to fully embrace development in a stress-free state. There are many events that can occur in a young child's life and while we may not be able to control this, we can help to build, and re-build foundations. While it is not listed as an ACE, we must also be aware that the educational experiences can also further sustain experiences of trauma, particularly if we do not engage in healing practices.

Trauma in early childhood is concerning because it can interfere with the development of different physiological systems such as handling and responding to stress and how we learn. Another issue is that trauma is not always that easy to spot or identify, and a child's behaviours, particularly as they get older may be associated to outdated views of behaviour, such as disobedience and defiance. Children deserve educators who will take the time to understand them, and who will not be swayed by quick-fix strategies that simply stop the expression of trauma but rather help to resolve it over time.

TYPES OF STRESS ACTIVITY

Using the types of stress below, think back to the culture of wellbeing in your setting and the wellbeing scales. What might you do differently to address each type of stress?

Positive stress	Brief increases in heart rate and a mild elevation in stress hormone levels. This may be activated by a minor change in routine, working out a problem or trying to navigate peer interactions. This type of stress is normal, expected, and healthy. It supports children's tolerance of challenges and problems and provides an opportunity to work through emotions and experiences.
High-intensity stress	A serious, temporary stress response with increased heart rate, elevation in hormone levels and may last longer than positive stress. Think of it like carrying a residue of stress and it needs to be shaken off. This type of stress is often best buffered by supportive relationships and responsive strategies.
Toxic stress	A prolonged activation of stress response systems has a physiological, hormonal and cognitive impact. This type of stress cannot just be shaken off but has a lasting impact on healthy development. There is often an absence of inconsistency in protective relationships and an effective set of strategies.

Wellbeing strategies

RULER to regulate

RULER was coined by Dr Marc Brackett and relates to key skills in emotional intelligence. Using this process enables adults to tune into children's emotional experiences and to recognise the impact of a feeling:

* *Recognising* emotions in oneself and others.
    "I can see that you are crying"
* *Understanding* the causes and consequences of emotions.
    "Your friend took your toy away and that made you feel upset"
* *Labelling* emotions with a nuanced vocabulary.
    "Am I right in thinking you are sad or is it anger?"
* *Expressing* emotions in accordance with cultural norms and social context.
    "It is okay to feel this way; I would also be sad if that happened to me."
* *Regulating* emotions with helpful strategies.
    "Next time, if you feel this way, you can come to me and ask for help?"

I have always used RULER in the moment, but when speaking with one of my university students, Daisy, she explained that in practice she found that when emotions are heightened it can be difficult to work through the steps in the moment. She aimed to provide timely responses but also recognised that following up once the dust settles can also be beneficial. She gave feedback to a group of students about her experiences and explained that the process could be used in flexible ways, and by returning to some of the skills, she was able to problem-solve her way through emotions with children and consider more personalised strategies.

Mood zones

It is important that children's feelings, emotions and moods are welcomed within the setting and that the environment is equipped to support children's different states of mood and mind. Children will rely on us to give them options for working through their moods. Think about the spaces within your environment, and how you model to children the way they can use the space to work through emotions and feelings.

A space to relax	A space to react and rupture	A space to retreat	A space to resolve and repair
Children need spaces that are universally relaxing, such as the reading area, but settings should also offer specific areas to support relaxation, such as a chill out cubby or zen zone.	It is important that we acknowledge that children will also need spaces where they can react without shame or punishment. Spaces that allow big body movements or noise are good so that a child can regulate that excess residue of stress. Some settings offer free flow spaces, but it is also important to consider how your indoor space opens up and allows expression of emotions and feelings.	As well as relaxation, children also need spaces where they can "escape" to, such as dens. Planning for areas where children can go under or behind is good and takes the pressure off them to recover quickly from strong emotions. These spaces should usually be "grown up" because the reality is that sometimes children want their own space.	A significant aspect of healthy emotional development is "rupture and repair". When things don't go to plan, children need time to be able to resolve this, and know that adults will be there to help them restore balance. You should consider how the different spaces within your environment cultivate repair such as emotional literacy, visuals or chatter spaces where children can spend quality time with adults.

(Continued)

(Continued)

Possible supports	Possible supports	Possible supports	Possible supports
Cushions and softening's so children can snuggle up. Have blanket baskets, or cubby holes where children can independently access objects of comfort. Weighted blankets or soft toys can reduce feelings of stress and anxiety. Lavender or other scented head wraps and cushions. Head and hand massagers. Noise-cancelling headphones or earmuffs. Access to calming music, or instruments. Visual relaxation reminders.	Box of sensory break ideas. Fidget toys or objects that support stimming, such as stress balls. Items to engage in heavy work, such as things to push, pull and lift. Paint rollers are great for supporting heavy work. Open spaces such as outdoors where they can physically engage and do not feel contained or trapped. Large scale equipment such as climbing frames, mini trampolines and wheeled vehicles.	Children like to burrow. Have a pop up tent within your main environment where children can hide, and nest away. Encourage children to build dens, and ask them about their favourite hiding spaces. Set up a sensory room or corner where children can go to when they need to find calm. If this is not possible, have sensory baskets, or embed sensory items such as lava lamps across your environment. Have a box of "Bear Hugs" in your environment so children can seek comfort, and offer bear hugs to children who need to retreat to a safe adult.	Use a wide array of emotions and feelings visuals so that children can find ways to communicate their feelings without having to talk. Use social stories, or personalised books to break down emotional experiences into more manageable chunks. Puppets can be beneficial for children when they feel distressed. Use a worry monster so children can express or talk about their feelings. Quality time with safe people. Emotional literacy and props. Have choice visuals so children can choose how to resolve and recover from stressful moments.

Reaction wall

 CASE STUDY

Melissa was working in a nursery that didn't always appear to be welcoming of children's feelings and emotions. Children were often told it was naughty to cry or "whinge" and that they needed to learn how to behave properly. Melissa spoke with the staff team about the importance of letting children explore their emotions. She asked if she could set up a reaction and responses wall that could be used when children wanted to express themselves. She used several visuals, such as a lion, an elephant, a bee, a tortoise and a mole. The idea was that children could point to the animal and decide what reaction that animal might have. For example, sometimes children would say they felt angry like a lion, and together Melissa and the child did the biggest lion's roar.

REACTION WALL
WHICH CREATURE DO YOU MOST RELATE TO?

Roaring like a lion	Buzzy like a bee	Slimy like a snail	Flighty as a butterfly

Angry Excited Annoyed	Anxious worried Enthusiastic	Tired Scared Calm	Bored Restless Energetic

Ideas	Ideas	Ideas	Ideas
• Roar like a lion • Movement & sensory breaks • Play	• Talk it out • Exercise and focus on breathing • Repeat calming actions • Stretch it out	• Talk it out • Cuddles • Relax • Sleep or listen to music	• Follow an interest • Get moving • Have a change of scenery • Work out a now and next routine

Make it magic

In their book *A Moving Child is a Learning Child*, Connell and McCarthy (2013) share a strategy known as the "Magic Door." The idea is that when each child arrives in the morning, they complete a "kinaesthetic action" that celebrates who they are. They see them themselves as going on an extraordinary adventure into the setting, and the space is somewhere they can be themselves, be a part of a community and know that doing it differently is absolutely okay. The Magic Door can be decorated, or the educator can simply focus on making the moment magical. They share a number of ideas, including:

- Give each child a musical instrument as they enter.
- Welcome the other children to come and give "high fives" to the child that enters.
- Tape balloons to the door, or add sensory lights.

- Dance into the room.
- Set a trail of pebbles or paper spots, so they follow the trail.
- Set up some climbing equipment to climb over.
- Jump like frogs.
- Hop.

Remember that the Magic Door should be inclusive, and you would base decisions on the needs of your children. You may also need to consider reasonable adjustments so that all children get to experience the adventure.

Moving through moods using sensory breaks

Mood Movements

In 2015, it was identified that 91% of children failed to meet the UK Physical activity guidelines (HSE, 2015). Sedentary behaviour or restricting movement can have significant impact on health and well-being.

Moving through moods recognise that children need to use their full bodies to regulate stress hormones, and as educators, we recognise that restricting movement can lead to further build ups of stress. Try the following to move through moods:

1. Have brain boost prompts so that when a child becomes stressed, you can offer to do an activity together, for example star jumps, dancing or heavy work for grounding.
2. Use tactile sensory items such as massage rollers which will support the child to become calm.
3. Try heart rests where the child lies on their back with their l egs elevated which eases pressure on the heart and nervous system.

Senses Key skills	Balance (vestibular) Key skills	Intuition (proprioception) Key skills	Power Key skills	Coordination Key Skills	Strength Key skills
Sight Hearing Smell Taste Touch	Posture Balance Alertness Concentration Stillness	Spatial awareness Mind free movement Strength	Strength Stamina Flexibility Agility	Midlines Dominance Body Rhythm Temporal Awareness	Positioning Pacing Pressure or force Eye coordination and tracking
Remove "visual noise" in stressful situations, for example, moving to a more neutral space Provide options for music, for example, playing a favourite song or calming sounds Provide subtle and calming scent within the environment, for example, opening a door to let the fresh air in, and encouraging mindful breathing Offer drinks or snacks. Stress eats up a lot of energy, and causes dehydration or hunger. In fact, sometimes, that is the source of stress.	Encourage different types of movement such as swinging, spinning and rolling. Vestibular driven movement is particularly useful for children who are disengaged, appear bored or restless. Build movement into learning so that the child is actively engaged, for example, action rhymes Do not expect long periods of sitting still.	Introduce burrito blankets, encouraging children to wrap themselves up when they feel physically "out of sorts." This will help them to feel safe and secure. Push and pull activities to help with physical, sensory integration and grounding, which will reduce feelings of anxiety or stress. Encourage the child to add pressure with self-hugging or massaging, which will reduce stress and provide self-soothing benefits.	Build in movement throughout the day and encourage risk play through scaffolding. Ensure appropriate challenges both indoors and outdoors and have a dynamic space that welcomes different types of movement. Use large paint rollers for heavy work exercise.	Provide opportunities to dance, and use expressive movement to work through emotions; for example, use different music to indicate different moods.	Introduce yoga poses for developing strength and build them into sensory breaks. Talk to children about the benefits, or how they might help. When children feel stressed, encourage them to lift their legs up high onto a chair, or wall to ease the pressure of stress on their bodies.

Mood Movements

Sensory Breaks

Stretch like a starfish

Grow as tall as a tree

Draw a rainbow

Do the puffer fish

Disco dance

Spider legs

Top Tips

- Use line drawings for children who may need support to process print
- Add to your brain boosts and ask the children for ideas
- If you do not have access to a printer, draw them out

Have a little box with the brain boosts inside, and explain to children that when they feel stressed, they can select a brain boost to release the stress in their busy body

Meditations

The Flower & The Candle Meditation

What we want to ensure for all children is that they can use strategies to manage their own feelings. This meditation experience is useful when children become stressed or worried, and helps to regulate and calm their breathing.

1. Ask the child to imagine that they have a flower in one hand, and a candle in the other.
2. Suggest thay they sniff up the flower, hold their breath for a moment, and then blow out the candle.
3. Repeat for as many times as desired.
4. The next time the child becomes upset, remind them of this technqiue so that theu can recognise moments of stress and respond to them.
5. It is also important to talk to children about what stress may feel like so that they understand why their breathing becomes busy.

CALMING CREATURES
THE SEA MEDITATION

I AM SILENT, I AM SILENT, IN THE SEA, IN THE SEA
I CAN FEEL THE SEA WEED, I CAN FEEL THE SEA WEED, IN
THE SEA, IN THE SEA
(WRIGGLE YOUR FINGERS)

I AM FLOATING, I AM FLOATING, IN THE SEA, IN THE SEA
I CAN FEEL THE FISH FLOW, I CAN FEEL THE FLOW, PAST
MY TOES, PAST ME TOES
(WIGGLE YOUR TOES)

(SIT UP)

I AM SWIMMING, I AM SWIMMING, IN THE SEA, THE SEA
I CAN FEEL THE WAVES CRASH, I CAN FEEL THE WAVES
CRASH, OVER ME, OVER
(WAVE YOUR ARMS)

HANDS TO THE HEART

Puppets

- Moriguchi, Sa-kata, Ishibashi and Ishikawa (2015) found that interaction with a doll or a puppet may have a significant impact on the development of thinking and feeling skills children aged between 3 to 5 years old. This includes flexibility in thinking, working memory and attentional control. If you are to use dolls or puppets, ensure that this is representative of children's identity and cultures.
- Korošec (2012) found that puppets act as a good mediator for communication and personal interaction amongst early years children. By using a puppet, you can support conflict resolution, understanding of difference and using the puppet as a gateway to play entry and friendships.
- Dunst (2012) found that the use of puppets can improve knowledge and change attitudes toward persons with disabilities.

Attachment support

Bubble messages *For separation anxiety*	Bubbles are great for sending and receiving messages, whether they be for affection, letting go of worries or to send hello's to the people we love.
	Simply ask the child to blow bubbles and to think about the message or to say it out loud. Equally, you can catch messages too. As a key person, you might send out bubbles as cuddles or happy thoughts.
	This experience will help children to feel close to those they love.
The Invisible string *For separation anxiety*	Use this idea to explain to children how they can remain close to those they love through the invisible string.
	Use a real piece of string if you have one, and each hold an end. Explain that between people exists the invisible string and how it keeps us close and connected. You can quite literally pull the heartstrings to remind you that your key person or loved one may not be physically close, but they are still emotionally close.
Worry dolls *For worries, anxiety or uncertainty*	Children often pick up on the anxiety of the adults around them. The key is not for us to suppress those feelings but to share openly with our children why it is okay to worry and what we might do to feel better. This can also be accompanied by making your own worry dolls and finding ways to talk about how to deal with worry.

(Continued)

(Continued)

We are Going on a Bear Hunt *Dealing with change, transition and challenge*	This book is essential for dealing with transitions and difficulties. Use the text to discuss the concept of facing changes and working our way through them.
Jar of strengths *Difficulties with managing feelings and behaviour*	Use a **Jar of Strengths** for children who struggle to manage their feelings and behaviours. Have an empty jar, and every time they show/ do a positive thing write or draw it on a post-it and put it in the jar. An alternative to this is to draw an outline of them on A3 paper and stick the post-it on the outline.
Holding in mind *For attachment insecurity*	If you have to leave the room, or the child has to go somewhere, ensure that you are transparent in your communication. For example, "I have to go on my lunch now, but I will be thinking of you while you also have your lunch, and I will be wondering how you are getting on. You can update me when I am back in an hour." This communicates the message that the child is important to you and helps the child to feel remembered and valued (You will be keeping them in mind).
Grounding activity *For fear and not feeling safe*	Find a place in the room where you can see the whole room, sit alongside each other, against a wall or on a chair with strong back support as this helps the child feel "grounded" and safer. Say something like let's have a good look around and check the room together. Talk about what you're seeing. "Look there's the painting corner/home corner," etc., "there's where everyone has hung their coats." Over time the time needed to do this will reduce and eventually won't be necessary at all. It helps to do this with any child who finds it difficult to settle, whether or not you think they feel unsafe. It helps them to acclimatise.
Rhythms *For fear and not feeling safe*	Give children really concrete, mechanical, rhythmic activities. These feel safe and soothing because they are logical and predictable. Activities such as:

- Sorting, copying, ordering and colouring in.
- Building things, sequencing objects or pictures.
- Rhythmical physical exercise and music.
- Providing areas where they can go inside something – to feel "contained" such as a playhouse area or a "den," even a large cardboard box.
- Activities involving missing links are good, for example: completing jigsaw puzzles and joining dots – these can feel therapeutic for the child.

Peer-mediated play

Children become aware of differences at quite a young age, and there can be a tendency to think that we need to ignore those differences. When speaking with an educator, she shared that she found herself saying "everyone's the same" even though she knew that the children within her setting were not the same. She felt overwhelmed when navigating discussions about differences, including skin colour, gender, abilities and disabilities. If we become hush-hush in our approach to difference, we might end up denying opportunities for children to learn more about each other, and finding commonalities and differences. Peer-mediated play is a good way to support all children and helps us strive towards children growing up with more inclusive ways of behaviour. For example, how often do you teach children the very strategies that you use when supporting children with developmental differences? Simple strategies can be shared and can help children to connect and find ways to play with each other.

 EDUCATOR'S VOICE

I had two children in my setting that used different visual systems, and I had noticed that the other children were really intrigued as to why Sammy had a visual board on the wall. I hadn't necessarily thought to provide much detail to the children, but one day a group of children began playing with the visual board and removed all the symbols. This messed up Sammy's routine, and she became quite distressed as I scrambled to create a bit more order. I saw this as an opportunity to teach the children about different ways of communicating and show how they needed to respect that the board belonged only to Sammy. I created a few sample resources, and we talked about why the pictures helped, and how there were lots of other different types of pictures within the environment.

Privacy spaces

It is still quite common that time out is used for punitive reasons when a child is dysregulated. This strategy can be quite harmful to young children, as the overarching message to the child is that we need them to comply to our expectations, and that we aren't necessarily interested in understanding their underlying need or reason for distress. Privacy spaces, however, can be useful for children with SEND because sometimes their behaviour is triggered by the environment and other children. Having spaces where the child can escape or nestle away is really important for their recovery from stress.

Photo credit: Emma Davis

Ableist strategies

When we think about children with SEND and the strategies that we may adopt for social, emotional and mental health, it is important to recognise that some of the boundary-based approaches can be quite ableist. For example, expecting a child to sit still in the early years is generally not developmentally responsive, but can be even harder for children with developmental differences. Over the recent years, we have seen attempts for a more responsive behaviour support system in settings, but alas, we still see strategies that do not take into account the child's social and emotional needs. I outline below just some of the ableism that currently exists within "behaviour management" approaches.

Golden rules and whole body listening

It is commonplace to see settings that promote the use of "golden rules," but these can often be quite exclusionary to children with SEND. More often than not, these rules become another thing that we have to keep reminding children, and they do not always transfer well to healthy development. Let's consider some examples:

1. Sit still

    It is well known that children should not be sitting still in the early years (Neaum, 2021). Movement underpins all other aspects of development, and is key to balance, coordination and thinking. Children sitting still is not evidence that they are paying attention, and the opposite has been found to be true; a fidgeting child is often a child developing focus. This rule can also be discriminatory against children who have SEND and rely on movement to feel integrated into their environment.

2. Listening ears, fingers on lips and being quiet

    While it is good to check that children have heard and understood us, we often focus too much on children being quiet and listening than engaging and using their "voices." Considering the prevalence of discussions around supposed word gaps, and speech, language and communication needs and whether we should we really be telling our children to be quiet?

3. Cross your legs

    It might be difficult to read, but this is a harmful practice, and places undue pressure on children to sit in positions that aren't natural or sustainable. Try doing this yourself for 10 minutes; how long can you maintain the legs crossed position? Your expectation of children should be something you can do too, but in most cases, educators struggle to sit in a specific position for more than a few minutes.

4. Put your toys away

    This most commonly happens during circle or carpet times and is usually targeted at the children trying to "sneak" in a car or small item to keep them occupied during circle time. We have to ask ourselves why this is a problem to us, because in most cases the toy represents that the circle time is not engaging for the child, and maybe we need to consider what we need to change to make it work or is simply an item to help the child pay attention. Fidget and fiddle items are great for helping children to pay attention.

Public behaviour charts

It can feel odd to be discussing behaviour charts in the contemporary early childhood environment, but there are still plenty of anecdotal examples of these charts being used to measure children's behaviour. They are harmful for a number of reasons; let's consider some of these:

1. They can create feelings of shame
   The easiest way to think about this is through the adult lens. Imagine going into your workplace and seeing a "staff behaviour" chart and at the bottom in the red zone was a picture of your face for everyone to see. Everyone would know you are the badly behaved one, and even when you are not at work you now get blamed for all the things that go wrong.

2. They do not motivate children to behave
   While the children who consistently get placed at the top of the chart may feel motivated to continue to succeed, for other children the continual feelings of failure may lead to them giving up altogether. As educators, we are essentially telling a child they are not good enough, and when someone doesn't feel good enough, the tendency can be to give up and to potentially live up to the label of being badly behaved.

3. It does not help to promote positive parent partnership
   Again, let's imagine that as a parent, you walk in to collect your child, and the first thing you are confronted with is the traffic light system of faces. It communicates a powerful message to parents about how you feel about their child, and unfortunately can create a very adversarial partnership.

What you can do instead:

- Catch them being good display (at the child's level) – have a sticky note board where children's contributions are welcomed and celebrated and embrace the small steps in behaviour.
- What we need to work on a collective board – behaviour is inevitable, so rather than single children out use behaviour support through a community lens. Talk to children about the behaviours you have observed, get their views and agree collectively on what you might need to work for a cohesive community.

SEND friendly spaces

Your environment should offer connection and belonging. Children and responsive adults should cultivate trust and togetherness. An early years environment belongs to the child, and we must continue to ask questions which help us to explore the perspective of the child:

1. Who are we?
2. Where do we come from?
3. Where do we see ourselves reflected and represented in this environment?
4. Where in this space do we learn about each other?
5. What opportunities do we have to learn about each other's strengths, and differences?
6. How am I able to contribute to this environment?
7. How does my family contribute?
8. How does the atmosphere of the setting create a sense of belonging?

- **Connection over compliance:** think about the routines across the day where behavioural issues increase. How necessary are these routines, and is the emphasis on compliance disrupting relationships? For example, is expecting children to sit for circle time valuable if they are disengaged?
- **Ditch golden rules:** many environmental rules place unrealistic expectations on children, and are often inappropriate for neurodivergent children. Use "agreements" instead which involves the children thinking about what keeps everyone happy, safe and thriving.
- **Hideaway:** hiding spots, and nooks and crannies so that children do not feel too exposed by the busy daily "bumblings."
- **Flexibility:** have familiar routines so children know what to expect, but balance this with flexibility so that it does not become too rigid or containing.
- **Be consistent:**
  - Adopt a buddy system for the key person so that care remains consistent.
  - Communicate changes and transitions to children, for example, using visual routines, reminders and a "who is here today" so that children can see which key people are available.
  - Inform children if there will be unfamiliar educators coming into the room.
  - Ensure consistency in handovers and plan additional adaptations for those children who may need more time to ease in, for example, some handovers may take place outside of the main room or the child may need longer to separate from the main carer.
  - Ensure that parents are not encouraged to do "disappearing acts" when a child is distressed. Create an established leave and return routine.
  - Encourage and welcome the use of transitional objects and comforters.

Conclusion

When supporting a child's social, emotional and mental health, we should be open to the possibility of "bumps in the road" and all children will face difficulties in navigating their emotional development. In most cases, this is to be entirely expected as it is part and parcel of learning. However, we must also be alert to underlying concerns or difficulties that are impacting on the child's wellbeing and participation.

While some children may simply need a set of supportive teaching techniques that provide them with boundaries, comfort and safety, others may require a much more targeted approach. It is important that educators develop a repertoire of attachment-aware and trauma-informed strategies and differentiate according to the child's needs. It is also important to recognise that it can take time for a child to work through SEMH difficulties. This does not indicate that you are failing to support, but rather, you recognise that a slow and steady approach to wellbeing means that children can fully integrate wellbeing strategies and self-regulation, which will help them beyond the early years phase.

 Read, watch and listen

The MEHRIT Centre of Self-Regulation by Stuart Shanker
https://self-reg.ca/

The Flourish Project by Wendy Ellyatt
https://www.flourishproject.net/partners.html

Watch Every Kids Needs a Champion by Rita Pierson
https://www.youtube.com/watch?v=SFnMTHhKdkw

Anna Freud National Centre for Children and Families
Early Years in Mind
https://www.annafreud.org/early-years/early-years-in-mind/

Centre on the Developing Child Harvard University
https://developingchild.harvard.edu/

Developing Essential Skills in Supporting Self-Regulation 3–4 years
https://www.suttontrust.com/wp-content/uploads/2020/01/Teacher
-Handbook-Self-Regulation-in-the-Early-Years.pdf

Adversity in Childhood is Linked to Mental and Physical Health
Throughout Life
https://www.bmj.com/content/371/bmj.m3048

4 | Physical and sensory needs

Defining physical and sensory needs

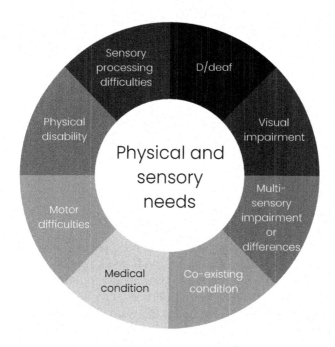

Physical needs can consist of a physical disability or a condition that impacts movement, such as a motor coordination disorder. Sensory development is intrinsically linked to movement and motor coordination, including proprioception and vestibular difficulties.

DOI: 10.4324/9781003138365-4

Sensory needs include D/deaf, visual and multi-sensory (vision and hearing) differences and impairments. Sensory needs also include sensory processing differences, and conditions that are often co-existent with other neurotypes such as autism.

Starting points

This chapter will consider sensory and physical development and its importance for overall healthy development. Imagine arriving at work and sitting down with your colleagues for a morning meeting. Suddenly, you experience a great big itch that you just have to scratch. When you go to scratch it, you are told to stop, and someone holds your hands down. You are told to stop fidgeting.

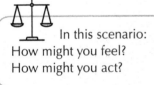
In this scenario:
How might you feel?
How might you act?

Introduction

Reflection

When I came to write a chapter that addressed physical development and movement, I was mindful of citing research about childhood obesity, sedentary behaviour and increased time on technology, which all can impact child health outcomes. While some of the research in this area is valuable, and should be considered thoughtfully, there are broader discussions about the ways in which these narratives can cause harm and which are rooted in ableism. Another concern is that parents are often blamed for children not having active enough lifestyles, yet it is within settings and schools that we see an increasing "bums on seats" agenda. I recently heard an educator say, "isn't it funny, we spend the earliest years of a child's life encouraging them to move and talk, and then spend the rest of their education telling them to sit still and be quiet." We all have a responsibility to ensure that children have a movement and sensory-rich experience, but this doesn't always mean being physically active through exercise but can encompass a range of embodied experiences.

Physical and sensory development

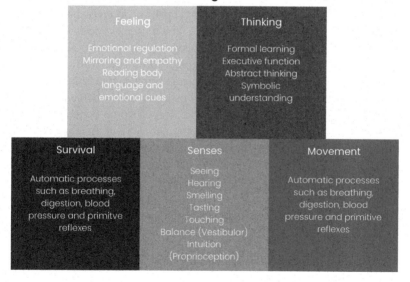

Building Blocks of Physical and Sensory Learning

Difficulties in survival senses or movement can impact feeling and thinking.

Feeling	Thinking
Emotional regulation Mirroring and empathy Reading body language and emotional cues	Formal learning Executive function Abstract thinking Symbolic understanding

Survival	Senses	Movement
Automatic processes such as breathing, digestion, blood pressure and primitve reflexes	Seeing Hearing Smelling Tasting Touching Balance (Vestibular) Intuition (Proprioception)	Automatic processes such as breathing, digestion, blood pressure and primitive reflexes

In his 2011 Ted Talk, Daniel Wolpert states that

we have a brain for one reason and one reason only; that's to produce adaptable and complex movements. Movement is the only way we have of affecting the world around us ... I believe that to understand movement is to understand the whole brain. And, therefore, it is important to remember that when you are studying memory, cognition, sensory processing, they're there for a reason, and that reason is action.

As you will see from the above image, there are foundational building blocks that we need in order to learn, and central to this learning is physical and sensory development. Our senses would not be very stimulated if we remained in one place, and so it is those early movement experiences that bring learning to life. According to Conell and Mccarthy, "movement unlocks the brain for learning" (2014, p. 16), and so we should actively encourage a movement-driven curriculum, including for children with SEND. The concerns over recent years about the reduction in how much children move, including long periods of remaining still referred to as sedentary behaviours is a concern, and it could be argued that the education system is failing children by having such an increased emphasis on "school readiness," which usually translates to compliance, sitting still, paying attention and following instructions. Ken Robinson argues that education now appears to operate from the waist up, and this is eroding our physical health and wellbeing. Similarly, Sally Neaum (2021) states that "children do not learn to sit still by sitting still" (p. 9), yet behaviour management approaches appear to want to keep children contained through reward, sanctions and conformity. In this chapter, we will think about what it means to be physically and sensorially engaged in our learning, and why we often mistake movement for "bad behaviours". When we hear the term "physical development," we might be tempted to think only of able-bodies, exercise or active movement, but it is a much more expansive process, and like all types of development it is diverse, unique and will sometimes differ.

Ableism and able-bodied children

Friedman and Owen (2017) state that ableism, like other "isms," such as racism and sexism, describes discrimination towards a social group and how certain ideals and attributes are valued or not valued (Wolbring, 2008). For example, able-bodied behaviours such as walking are considered more socially valuable than someone moving by way of a wheelchair. For a disabled child, we have to consider how much value we place on their identity and development, but also how wider frameworks sustain the existence of ableism. We will see across this chapter that physical development is often described through an ableist lens, and a preference for able-bodied existence. There are also harmful narratives about obesity, physical activity and sedentary behaviour that position the child or parent at fault with little recognition that there is a societal responsibility to support healthy development.

When we think of movement, we should avoid doing this through an "able-bodied" lens and recognise that all humans, including those with physical disabilities, have forms of movement that will be very important to their health and wellbeing. I recall once being part of a sports day where the headteacher suggested that a child in a wheelchair not take part because none of the activities were suited to a wheelchair user. Yet having worked closely with this child, they never stopped moving and loved to dance. To know that it had not occurred to the headteacher to expand her repertoire of ableist physical activities was very worrying and suggests that we need to think more expansively about the definition of movement.

Physical development and physical activity

One of the difficulties with physical activity and development is that it is traditionally discussed from a medical model perspective, and so perceptions of health are represented as an absence of illness or impairment. This immediately places those children with physical disabilities in the deficit position, and research has found that these perceptions can result in fewer opportunities or expectations for disabled children and reduce engagement in health-promoting behaviour (Friedman and Owen, 2017). Physical development is often quite narrowly defined as movement, and expenditure of energy, but the below redefines the definition as follows:

> Physical activity involves people moving, acting and performing within culturally specific spaces and contexts, and influenced by a unique array of interests, emotions, ideas, instructions and relationships.
>
> (Piggin, 2020)

This definition accounts for the idea that personal lived experiences actually shape physical activity abilities. We must also be mindful that "Physical activity is a deeply affective, emotional activity. The spectrum of emotions in physical activity range from joy and feelings of empowerment" (Light, 2003) and so we should ensure that we have an all-encompassing understanding of movement that benefits all children.

Physical play

According to Scholes and Mindell (2016), 91% of children in the early years fail to meet the Chief Medical Officers Recommendations in the UK Physical Activity Guidelines. This issue only worsens as children progress through primary school, and Public Health England suggests that children's activity levels drop by 40% across the primary phase. These statistics alone suggest that the early years and education systems have a prime responsibility to provide play-rich opportunities, and that we must push back against a "bums on seats" mentality as a feature of learning. The late Dr Len Almond (2016) proposes a framework for movement which consists of:

* Object play
   Children are driven by a desire to explore and to engage in enquiry-based learning. They will experiment with lots of different objects and develop key skills such as hand movements, manipulating, moving, throwing, catching, constructing and interacting with lots of different objects. If a child has a physical or sensory needs, you will need to consider how object play is supported and key skills developed. For example, you might make use of a resonance board, which is a plywood

board designed to reduce the chaos of noise for a child who has a vision impairment. Objects can be placed on the board for exploration and offer a space in which the child can actively learn in a safe way. The resonance boards can also be useful for children with sensory processing differences, and who may need low arousal play.

- Exercise play

    Being physical underpins our wellbeing, mental health and ignites feelings of joy. Children should be actively encouraged to engage in exercise, and this might include rough and tumble, climbing, running, chasing, wheeling, games, heavy work, pushing, pulling and digging. It is important not to assume that if a child is physically disabled that they cannot engage in exercise play, and this will rely on your thoughtful judgements and reasonable adjustments, for example, working with the child's areas of physical strength. For example, if the child is in a wheelchair or has adaptive equipment, try ten-pin bowling, obstacle courses or yoga.

- Expressive movement patterns

    Our environments must absolutely link to creative and expressive movement. Dancing, partying, singing and engaging in gymnastics is key to joyful movement. Educators should consider those activities and experiences where they may restrict movement, such as circle times, and consider how they can integrate movement into everyday practices. As part of a child's settling-in, one of the key questions to ask is about their favourite music, and you can then build a soundtrack based on the sounds that get children moving and expressing themselves. Bhat and Srinivasan (2013) found that music activities and experiences can lead to positive emotions, particularly for children with disabilities. Again, do not assume that because a child may have hearing difficulties or loss that they cannot enjoy the vibrations, and indications of sound.

- Outdoor education

    An outdoor education is key to a child's opportunities for movement and has a wide range of wellbeing benefits too. We should never see the outdoors as simply a place to run off energy, but as a learning space. For many disabled children, the outdoors can be preferred because it feels less restrictive and overwhelming.

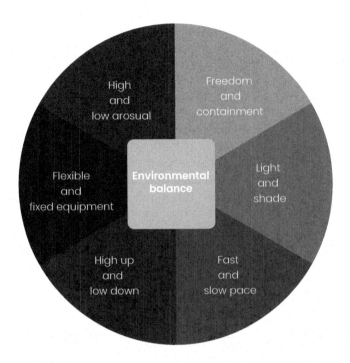

For children with SEND, educators will need to consider how these opportunities are available to all children and adapted so that children can fully participate in activities and experiences.

Risky play

Dare to play

The benefits of risky play are well-cited, but when it comes to children with SEND, educators can become quite averse to providing opportunities for challenge and risk. The crucial step is to risk assess and plan for supports such as scaffolding. Risk play should take place in the context of a secure relationship, and the educator should know when the risky play falls outside of the child's zone of development. It is also important to think about risk as per the child's individual abilities. For example, for one child, jumping from a height might be an appropriate form of risk play, but for another child it might be exploring different sensory materials for the first time. We should not see risk play as something dangerous; rather, it is the moment in which a child moves beyond their own zone of comfort.

Unruly or regulated risks

How do you feel when a child does the following?

- Climbs the wrong way up the slide.
- Climbs on furniture.
- Runs indoors.

We can often disrupt play with our desire to control or restrict children's movements based on our idea of early childhood spaces being used in a functional or practical way. As adults, we tend to use spaces this way, and this expectation can filter down to the child. The issue with this is that it often stifles potentially important learning opportunities. For example, climbing up a slide allows the child to see the world from a new and novel perspective while supporting his core strength and muscles. Rather than telling a child to stop, we should use this moment to support their knowledge of risk and safety. If a child is about to come down, we might encourage the child to problem-solve or role-play some solutions. Similarly, the fascination for children to move in one way in indoor spaces often makes no sense. If children are indicating a need to run, as well as ensuring they have adequate space outdoors, we should rethink our indoor environment, and whether it allows for enough movement. It is often children with SEND who come under fire for not using spaces in the way we would like, and again we see this behaviour simply being viewed as part of their delay. However, if we spend more time listening to those play cues, we can provide opportunities for learning, and see our environment as a crucial support system for SEND.

My space, your space

One of the most frequent discussions I have when supporting educators about SEND support is the layout and appropriateness of the early year's environment. Discussions around play spaces can quickly become complicated as we navigate concepts such as ownership, rules, educator identity, aesthetics and purpose. In recent years we have seen a momentous shift towards aesthetics, particularly the idea of moving away from colourful layouts and plastic resources. The rise of social media and teaching accounts has also led to a vast increase in interior-based classrooms and everyone proclaiming that "neutral is best." I have even been subject to some horror stories of teachers shaming others for the use of a plastic storage box over a wicker basket. While I embrace a natural environment, I think that we are often steered away from what really matters in the early years, and that is environments that reflect the actual children within them. While aesthetics is an important talking point for children with SEND, there is much less discussion about how children occupy, move and behave in these spaces.

I recently saw a tweet from a teacher who expressed that she had become tired of the environment shaming within education. She proclaimed: "do you, it's *your* classroom." On the one hand, I could totally see her frustration because social media has indeed become a space to showcase our pedagogy and ideas, which can in turn add increased pressure to those who are at different stages. On the other hand, however, it highlights that we as educators often completely overlook an important factor … it is not *our* classroom … it belongs to our children. Part of the issue with the inclusive environment is that it often doesn't actually end up belonging to the child, and the child becomes negatively contained by it. If we are to encourage children to fully embrace and embody the environment through movement and learning, we need to remember that children are not entering our world in the early years environment; we are entering theirs. And our role within that is to reflect who they are in the spaces, places, attitudes and practices.

Sensory development

Connell and McCarthy explain that "In early childhood, the brain is so hungry for information, you can see the senses in action all day, every day – and especially in the things that encourage children to move" (2014). Children thrive when they are in an environment that ignites their full range of senses. Skills such as balancing, coordination, and using strength all begin with a body that is seeking sensory information and bringing all that information together. Most educators are aware of the five senses of touch, sight, hearing, tasting and smelling, but the sensory system is much more complex, and also includes proprioception (balance) and vestibular sense (intuition).

What type of sensory experiences do you think might tip the wellbeing scales? How often do you check in with the children to see how they are managing daily sensory input?

RAISING A SENSORY SMART CHILD ACTIVITY

In this section, think about the different senses, and how you support them within your early years environment:

The senses

- The tactile or sense touch is the very first to develop in the womb and is the biggest sensory organ in the body (Biel and Peske, 2009). Try it out: count how many things you touch in the space of a few minutes. You will notice, we are constantly in-touch with the world, and it is one of our great sensory communicators.
  How do you create touchy-feely spaces for children?
- Sight is a survival sense as it alerts us to danger or allows us to weigh up risk and soothes us when we are looking for safety.
  What do children see when they enter your setting? Is the layout and structure of the environment clear, and does it make sense? And, most importantly, do children see themselves in your environment? How representative is your space?

- "Listening is a whole-brain, whole-body experience that connects us to our environment and is the pre-cursor to interaction, speaking, reading and writing" (Hanscom, 2019).

  Do you develop communication friendly spaces? Is noise managed effectively so that children experiment with listening within different spaces.

  Listening is also an emotive experience that allows us to feel "in-tune," for example, listening to calming music when stressed.

- Smell is also primitive and alerts us to danger and is connected to our emotions, hence why smells remind us of memories, people and time. Our experience of smell sends messages to the brain, which activates emotions, motivation and pleasure (limbic system).

  How is smell managed within your setting? Do children have adequate ventilation? Do you ask children about smells, and check likes and dislikes?

- According to Biel and Peske (2009), smells quite literally play on our feelings.

- Taste which is closely connected with smell tells us information about the environment, hence why babies and young children take everything into their mouths. It is a form of sensory exploration.

  Refer to the "Read watch and listen" section below to find further ideas for supporting taste.

Proprioception

If we want a curriculum that jumps for joy, we must commit to movement, and limit our use of the following statements:

"Sit still!"
"Stop fidgeting!"
"Calm down!"
"Stop moving!"
"Pay attention!" (when we assume movement means low attention)

- Proprioception is the ability to position yourself in space and becomes intuitive. Through our joints, muscles, tendons, ligaments and the inner ear, we develop "mind free movement," which is the ability to understand spatial awareness (Neaum, 2019).
- It is the process of understanding your bodily positions and movements without having to look. We often take this type of movement for granted, but our proprioception is at work all the time, for example, knowing how much pressure to apply to something fragile or knowing where your body is in space when you sit down without falling off your chair.
- Our body senses position and movement, and because this sense involves so many aspects of proprioception, for us to develop we have to exercise all the different components.
- Always remember that the "body needs to move to think" (Robinson, 2014), and if we want children to be fully engaged with their learning, they need opportunities to be physically, emotionally and socially active.

Vestibular

- Often the most overlooked sense but vitally important is our sense of balance known as the vestibular sense.
- There are little hairs in our inner ear, and when we move our body and head in all different directions, the fluid in the inner ear moves back-and-forth, stimulating these little hairs. This stimulation provides us with information about our position in space and helps us to navigate with control and ease.
- You will notice when people have ear infections or children have glue ear, that their balance can become unstable. They will often report feeling very disorientated, and this is because the body is not getting enough information.
- Balance supports coordination, body awareness and skilful balance, all skills which are needed for later reading, writing, focus, attention and emotional regulation.

- Developing balance is preparedness for academic learning, so lots of movement in the early years is never wasted.

With all these sensory systems at work, we also need to consider how they might work together. This is a process known as sensory integration.

Did you know?

There is a lesser-known sense known as introception. This helps you to understand and feel what is going internally, for example, identifying hunger or different feelings. For children with SEND, they may have trouble figuring out their internal experiences, and may therefore struggle to process their senses and to emotionally regulate. Educators should support children to identify introception, for example, talking about what hungry might feel like, or anger and link this to the physical sensations (Understood.org).

Sensory integration

Sensory integration is quite simply, how we absorb all the sensory information and organise it to develop our understanding. The senses actively work together to build a sensory picture, and therefore help our bodies to respond appropriately. For example, imagine a child is playing and he smells lunch, this will likely engage his sense of sight to locate where the smell is coming from, the child can then decide if he will move to physically locate the food, and with this sensory information make a decision whether to move over to where the food is. Hanscom (2016) describes it as taking all the puzzle pieces and putting them together to create a bigger picture. Sensory integration is an all-too-common difficulty with many different types of SEND, and when a child is unable to put that picture together, they will often have to put more effort in, which can become tiring, overwhelming and frustrating. This can be particularly difficult if the sensory integration is not understood, and some of the child's reactions are put down to acts of misbehaviour and defiance.

Sensory processing differences and difficulties

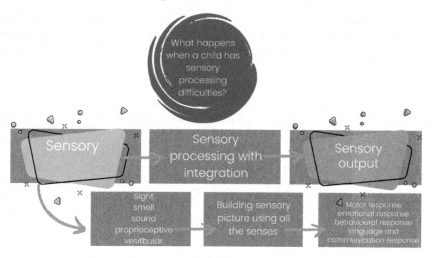

Biological and physiological systems can be quite overwhelming to consider when we think of child development, but for many children with SEND, sensory processing differences and difficulties are quite common. The most straightforward way of exploring the sensory system is through the three distinct phases as outlined by Murray-Slutsky and Paris (2005):

- Sensory stimulus relates to the information we take in through our senses (for example, visual, auditory, tactile, proprioceptive and vestibular).
- Central processing is how we use all our sensory information to create a sensory picture.
- Sensory output is how we filter out that sensory information through meaningful motor, language, behavioural or emotional responses.

The operation of these three phases together leads to sensory integration. And so, sensory processing difficulties emerge when one or more of these phases does not integrate with the others. It can be difficult to fathom how uncomfortable sensory processing difficulties can feel, particularly as they can be quite specific. There are numerous videos on social media to try and illustrate the feelings of being overwhelmed and overloaded, but they do not always fully convey the intensity and the ranges of sensory experiences. The truth is that we all have a sensory profile, and we will have different levels of tolerance. Have you ever experienced the following?

- Extreme sensitivity when brushing your teeth.
- Feeling shocked when an unexpected sound occurs, such as an ambulance with sirens.
- Discomfort from a plastic tag being left in your clothing.
- Your hair blowing into your mouth when it is windy.

These relatively minor experiences can really interfere with our concentration and our irritability levels, and in most cases, because we can see the cause, we can stop the sensation. With sensory processing difficulties, there can be a whole array of sensory sensitivities, including those that are hyper, meaning over-sensitive, and hypo, meaning under-sensitive.

How does SPD disrupt daily life?

- High distractibility, with difficulties maintaining attention.
- Challenges with remaining on task.
- An unusually high or low activity level.
- Frequent tuning out or withdrawing.
- Intense, out-of-proportion reactions to challenging situations and unfamiliar environments.
- Impulsiveness, with little or no self-control.
- Difficulty transitioning from activity to activity, or situation to situation.
- Rigidity and inflexibility at times.
- Perceived carelessness.
- Discomfort in group situations.
- Social or emotional difficulties.
- Broader developmental and learning difficulties.
- Trouble handling frustration, tendency to tantrum longer and more intensely than other children do, and more difficulty returning to a calm state.
- Problems transitioning from an alert, active state to a calm, rested state (for example, difficulty falling asleep or waking).

(Biel, 2005, p. 13)

Types of sensory processing difficulties

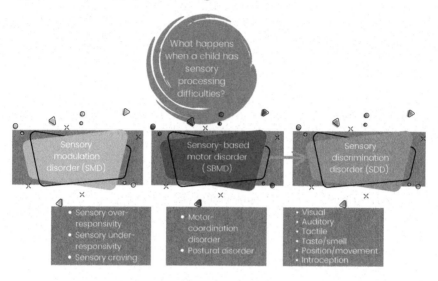

There are thought to be three patterns of sensory processing disorder as outlined here:

Sensory Modulation Disorder (SMD)

This refers to how sensory information is organised and how the nervous system responds to information. The response is often disproportionate to the experience, for example, being over-responsive or under-responsive to information. Children may be sensory seekers or avoiders.

Example: Mark attends a school nursery which he appears to enjoy very much. The teachers have noticed that when the school bell goes off each day, Mark will scream very loudly and cover his ears. It will take him a long time to calm down.

Explanation: Mark struggles to regulate the unexpected sensory input of the school bell, and this ignites his nervous system.

Support idea: provide Mark with a visual reminder each day so that he knows that the sound is coming and provide him with noise-cancelling headphones to block out the sound.

Sensory-Based Motor Disorder

This refers to postural or movement-based challenges, for example, being accident-prone or disorientated in movement. Children may go on to be diagnosed with developmental coordination disorder previously referred to as dyspraxia.

Example: Claire is struggling with self-care skills and will often knock items over, such as her drink at snack time. When fastening up her jacket, she will often misplace her hand or struggle to locate the buttons.

Explanation: Claire has not fully developed "mind free movement" and struggles to identify herself and her surroundings within a physical space, leading to disorientation.

Support idea: provide hand-under-hand support for Claire so that the adult can guide her actions, for example, help to pour a drink.

Sensory Discrimination Disorder

This refers to troubles in perceiving sensory information, for example, not knowing the properties of an object, not understanding the physical force or being able to gauge variable sensory information.

Example: Harriett loves to play with her peers but is having some difficulty with friendships as she will often not realise her own strength and will squeeze her friends too hard or run into them.

Explanation: this too is linked to "mind free movement" and "power" and demonstrates that Harriett does not have the sensory input to identify weight or different properties, meaning she shows less awareness of her movements.

Support idea: provide visual reminders or cues for Harriett to use "gentle hands" or to test things out before going full force.

ACTIVITY

Play four different songs at the same time on YouTube and try to have a conversation with a colleague. How did it feel? For a person with sensory integration difficulties, the sense of being overwhelmed can be triggered by everyday sounds. For example, in a preschool room, the sound of lots of children, music and environmental sounds can all interfere with processing.

Wellbeing strategies

Sensory-rich play

There can sometimes be an assumption that children with SEND either love or hate sensory-based experiences, and this can sometimes lead to hesitation from educators to explore different ideas. According to Gascoyne, it is about developing an understanding of the individuals' sensory preferences and planning accordingly. In her book on *Sensory Play*, she recommends the following:

Aim for "just right"

Many children with development differences and conditions can become over- and under-stimulated, but through careful observation, educators should identify when a child might be open to sensory exploration. By gradually introducing experiences and resources, educators can build up a personalised "sensory diet" for each child.

Decide on what you can offer as a "main meal" and "sensory snack"

We each will work in different types of provisions, and so it is important to think realistically about the types of sensory diet you can offer. Whereas some settings will be able to have sensory rooms as their "main meal," others may use the outdoor space. We can also often stop using resources such as treasure baskets as children become older, but they are still an essential resource that can be used throughout the foundation years.

See further reading in this chapter for a full description of sensory diets:

https://www.communityplaythings.co.uk/learning-library/articles/sensory -play-for-children-with-sen

Sensory treasure and discovery baskets

> The treasure basket concept was inspired by Elinor Goldschmied many years ago but has caught on throughout the United Kingdom and increasingly in other countries as well. It is a simple yet profound idea, opposing the trend to give commercial plastic toys to babies by providing them instead with a richer sensory experience.
>
> (Community Playthings)

- Treasure baskets consist of exploratory items in different types of wicker baskets.
- They enable young children to have the sensorial exploration of different items.
- The baskets are usually organised by theme, for example, fabrics, wood, metal and textures.
- The treasure basket should be within a child's reach and can be rotated or scattered across an environment.

Hand-under-hand to hand-over-hand, aka tactile modelling

This statregy is subject to much debate due to many believeing that it can disrupt the autonomy and consent of the child. I am inclined to agree that this is a strategt that can be misused, and so when offering tactile support, we must always do this in a child-led way. There are, however, a range of disabilities where exploration may provoke anxious feelings for a child and the comfort of touch is welcomed. For example, during play, a child with multi-sensory differences may be reluctant to experiment with materials or toys. The hand-under-hand technique should be a gentle way of introducing, supporting and scaffolding a child to engage with something new. By placing their hand on top of your own, they can be guided by you, and have the option to remove their hand if they do not feel comfortable. As the educator and child build confidence in this type of exploration, the hands may switch so that the child gets more direct access to the materials. It is important, however, that the child knows they can move their hand away. Eventually, however, it is the educator who pulls their hand away as the child becomes more independent.

A very good demonstration of hand-under-hand technique can be found on the SENSE YouTube channel, just search: making play inclusive – hand-under-hand communication.

Playing at different heights

According to Clemens and Lincoln (2018) active free play is associated with healthy physical growth, increased concentration and the development of social skills. While our environment should offer predictability and familiarity for children with a range of physical and sensory needs, it is important that they are enabled to play at different heights, which requires different uses of the body and gives the child the chance to see the world from different perspectives. It is not uncommon to still see early childhood environments that have a lot of desks with chairs, especially towards the latter end of the foundation stage. This is concerning given the growing issue of sedentary behaviour in childhood (Neaum, 2019). Children, however, need to be able to engage with the following:

• Ensuring some desks allow for freestanding play rather than expecting children to sit down for long periods.
• Having floor time experiences, and clearly defined spaces for playing lower down.

- Designing "nooks and crannies" spaces for children to hide away.
- Use furniture in unusual ways to encourage exploration, for example, taping paper under the desk for upside-down mark-making.
- Ensuring there are spaces for gross-motor stimming behaviours, such as spinning and rocking.

SAFE activities

It is important to ensure that when children experience sensory processing differences and difficulties, we plan with their emotional safety and wellbeing in mind. For children to learn, they need to feel safe, so this acronym perfectly suits those children who may not have developed full sensory integration. Activities should be:

Sensory-Motor based so that they can begin to sync up their sensory experiences with movement. According to Kranowitz (2016), "the more sensory-motor experiences young children have, the more easily they learn to function in daily life" (p. 10). Using their whole bodies enables them to build a better sensory picture, and to come to understand how they might need to do it differently, or what to be aware of.

Appropriate activities and experiences are important. When working with young children, you will find that developing a good sensory profile means that you can plan and scaffold activities that suit this profile.

Fun activities that meet the child's interests are also important, and we should not be introducing experiences that may be too over- or underwhelming. It is quite common for educators to be reluctant to engage in sensory-based activities when a child has differences in this area because the emotional response and stress can feel daunting. Knowledge is power here and understanding that it isn't about teaching the child to tolerate that which does not suit their learning needs but engages them in fun and capacity building ways.

Easy to set up, Environmentally friendly, Emotionally satisfying and Economical. The idea of a SAFE activity is to be able to provide ample opportunities for children to develop key skills through play, so if it is a "one off" or expensive, it may be hard to sustain. By ensuring that plans for SAFE activities are easy enough to plan and do, and work in the space you are in, this makes those activities being integrated into daily life, more of a possibility.

(Adapted from Kranowitz, 2016)

SAFE activities should always be stopped if a child indicates a small window of tolerance.

In her book *Supporting Children With Social, Emotional and Mental Health Needs in the Early Years* (2021), Sonia Mainstone-Cotton provides several activities that support the SAFE principles, these include:

Homemade playdough: you can introduce children to different smells, colours and textures, building their sensory diet up.

Sensory tubs: these can enable you to focus on different properties or themes, for example, seasonal sensory tubs, different sounding textures or opposites such as hard/soft and loud/quiet.

Barefoot play: using different textures for the child to walk on, which will build sensory integration and balance. For example, walking on bubble wrap, crunchy paper or different textured rug squares.

Sensory havens

Sensory havens are spaces for children who may become overstimulated, for example, as a result of sensory processing disorder. Safe havens are good places to co-regulate and to support the development of self-regulation and can be helpful during busy nursery days. We often imagine separate rooms or sensory spaces with expensive sensory equipment, but these areas can also be designed on a realistic budget. Some ways to develop a sensory haven:

- Choose a separate space, or corner, nook or cranny, and if you don't have any of these consider a tent, den or even a very large cardboard box.
- Add some sponge or tactile materials to the wall.
- Have a material box with different textures, and weighted blankets.
- Vibrating mats.
- Bean bag chairs.
- Sensory Baskets with key sensory soothing items such as fidgets and earmuffs.
- Soothing lighting.
- Music.

Photo credit: Joanna Ludlam

As children become familiar with the space, incorporate these items across the environment so that children can opt to use these items independently.

Photo credit: Ronnie's Pre-School

Environment scanning

Children with SEND can experience stress due to environmental triggers. It is crucial that when a child is distressed, we carry out environment scanning, and consider whether adaptations can ease the experience of stress. Consider the following:

Visual	Auditory	Tactile	Smells
Can strip lighting be turned off, or dimmed? Is there any clutter that can be removed? Are there spaces and enclosures where a child can "escape" to? Is there a lot of movement going on around the setting? Are there lots of children around?	Are there any low-frequency sounds or buzzing that could be irritating? What are the acoustics like? What are the intonations of voices? Try calm and smooth rather than loud and directive. Is there loud music or noise pollution from any spaces? Can the child "escape" the noise climate, for example, going outdoors?	Does the child have a safe distance between themselves and others? Does the child welcome or reject touch? If the child welcomes, try patting or rubbing their back. If they reject, gently pat or rub your own leg to create a rhythm and calm. Provide softening such as cushions and blankets as an option. Offer sensory soothing resources such as "squishies" or playdough.	Are there any powerful smells in the space? Is there a mixture of smells that could be overwhelming? Is there an outlet for fresh air and spaces? Can you open or close windows dependent on where the smell might be coming from? Do you make use of blinds to limit direct sunlight or overheating?

Heavy work

According to the Child's Therapy Play Centre (2019), heavy work is a strategy used in therapy to target the sense of proprioception. The joints are where the receptors for proprioception are. When we participate in heavy work activities, messages are sent from receptors in our joints to receptors in our brainstem. This helps us to feel grounded and can also be soothing due to the repetitive nature. Heavy work can be utilised in the moment quite freely.

Robin referred to as "Bobbins" (2 years old) has social communication differences and sensory integration difficulties. He is an energetic and active child, and despite processing difficulties, is eager to engage in movement-based activities, including heavy work:

Spaced learning (sensory breaks)

The brain isn't designed to focus for long periods of time, and so it is important that we space out

Photo credit: Hayley Murphy

Photo credit: Hayley Murphy

Photo credit: Hayley Murphy

focused learning with movement. Research suggests that when a child has opportunities to move in between adult-directed learning, they can better consolidate what they are being taught, and self-regulate to re-engage. Ideally, learning should involve movement but for specific moments of focus, ensure that this is spaced out. Many educators are familiar with the concept of a sensory break. The premise is that the child stops what they are doing to engage in an energetic or intentional movement activity such as jogging on the spot, spinning, stretching or dancing.

Strategies to avoid

Sitting still

Children under no circumstances should be expected to sit for long periods of time. This can actually be more detrimental to their development as it places pressure on developing muscles and joints. Ensure that your curriculum is as active as possible. Where children have physical differences and difficulties, ensure reasonable adjustments allow for different types of movement.

 DID YOU KNOW?

Educators will often think of self-stimulating behaviours, also to referred to as stimming, as a negative or concerning behaviour. However, in recent years, the autistic community have spoken out in defence of stimming as a sign of excitement and happiness. The concern from autistic individuals is that stimming is often viewed as something to be stopped as opposed to a form of communication that can also be positive (Kapp et al., 2019).

SEND friendly spaces

- **Reasonable adjustments are prioritised**
  - There is a plan for physical accessibility.
  - Staff ensure that resources are easily accessible to all children, e.g. in low-level. baskets or containers clearly marked with a photo or object of reference related to the content.
  - The setting has accessible changing facilities, and all staff are available to deal with accidents.
- **Sensory safety**
  - Consider the acoustics within the environment, and aim to reduce noise with softenings and partitioning.
  - Consider sensory triggers, for example, positioning an area where children play on the ground next to tables and chairs where lots of noises can occur.
  - Weighted blankets, and noise-cancelling resources are available.
  - Have opportunities for different types of movement, and always observe for sensory soothing movements rather than contain children.
  - Provide a place where the young person can take themselves for time out, for example, a small tent or cabin bed. Young people affected by sensory sensitivity often find dark and enclosed spaces calming.
  - Large climbing frames, trampolines, chutes and swings.
  - Small water features can be extremely calming or give something to distract when things are difficult for a young person. Likewise, small wind chimes, musical chimes, light reflector toys or spinning toys may be both aesthetic and enjoyable.
- **Outdoor space**
  - There is accessible outdoor space that has a variety of activities and equipment to meet the developmental needs of all children.
  - Can children indicate when they are overwhelmed? The big button strategy can be helpful, which children can press when they are overwhelmed.
  - Minimise clutter so that children can focus.
  - Can children receive bear hugs when they need to centre themselves?
  - Mirror strategies for the child such as squeezing parts of the face and cheeks for sensory regulation.
  - Do you provide snuggle spaces for children?
  - Staff ensure the provision of facilities to enable personal care for children who may not be toilet trained or who need health care support.
  - Use heavy work strategies for emotional and sensory regulation.
  - The use of sensory toys, chews and sensory regulating items that belong to the child.

Conclusion

Despite the many examples in this chapter that highlight the importance of movement within physical and sensory development, we still exist within an education system that educates children out of their movement in favour of sitting still and focusing. At the time of writing this book, we are coming out of a third national lockdown in England and beginning to see the headlines about the detrimental impact the pandemic has had on children's development. One of the initiatives introduced by the Department for Education is the introduction of behaviour hubs into schools. The focus of these hubs is to get children back into shape, and when I say this I don't mean with plenty of time, movement, play and empathy. No, one, headteacher proudly states that he wants his children to focus 100% of the time, remaining silent and not talking off task. Within these pages, what we will have hopefully come to understand is that children cannot be disciplined into one size fits all conformity. Imagine the impact of these expectations on a child with ADHD, or in fact any child. We must push back on these agendas to reduce children into compliance, and as Descartes declares, "nothing can exist within the mind, it isn't allowed to exist within the body" (Descartes).

Read, watch and listen

Making Play Inclusive: A Guide for Settings by SENSE
https://www.sense.org.uk/get-support/support-for-children/play
-toolkits/

Leicestershire Sensory Processing Resource Pack
https://resources.leicestershire.gov.uk/sites/resource/files/field/pdf
/2017/9/21/early_years_sensory_processing_resource_pack.pdf

A Parent's Guide to Sensory Processing by Cerebra
https://cerebra.org.uk/download/sensory-processing/

The Out of Sync Child Video Series by Carol Kranowitz
https://out-of-sync-child.com/talks/

A Moving Child is a Learning Child (Chapter Sample)
https://www.freespirit.com/files/original/A-Moving-Child-Learning
-Child-preview-1.pdf

Ready to Learn Introception Kit
https://www.education.sa.gov.au/sites/default/files/ready-to-learn
-interoception-kit.pdf

5 | Speech, language and communication needs

Defining speech, language and communication needs

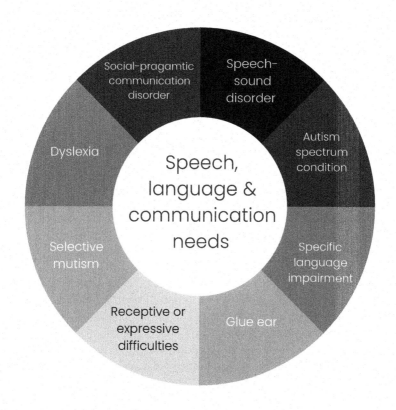

DOI: 10.4324/9781003138365-5

Children with speech, language and communication needs (SLCN) can have difficulty communicating with others. This can be for a range of reasons, and it is important to understand that the initial signs of delay may lead to alternative forms of communication such as sign language, visual systems and augumentive and alternative forms of communication. Children with SLCN may have difficulty understanding or expressing their needs and may not relate to neurotypical social rules of communication. Children may have specific or multiple SLCN needs, and this may impact on the other broad areas such as physical and/or sensory needs. SLCN includes social communication disorder that is characterised by difficulties with the use of verbal and non-spoken language for social purposes. Primary difficulties are in social interaction, social cognition and pragmatics. SLCN are usually present in autism, ADHD and dyslexia.

STARTING POINTS

Helpful or harmful?

Imagine being in a situation where you were unable to speak, and someone said the following. Would you find this helpful or harmful?

- Use your words
- I don't understand you, try again
- Can you say it properly?
- Speak up

What might you find more helpful?

Introduction

There is increasing evidence that the prevalence of speech, language and communication needs is quite high amongst children who also experience social, emotional and mental health difficulties. Difficulties in both these areas can have a significant impact on a child's participation and can lead to further challenges in learning and participation. If we consider a child who does not feel understood, and whose language does not "match" that of their peers, we might hazard a guess that this increases the likelihood of not being able to make friends, express interests or wants, and may not have their needs met. The combination of these left unsupported will only lead to greater difficulties and becomes harder still if the child has a developmental condition that signifies long-term differences in how they will communicate and relate to the world around them.

The idea that communication consists of much more than spoken language is well known to early educators, but oftentimes there are missed opportunities to fully embrace the richness of communicating differently. We often hear of headlines regarding word gaps and the long-term impact of speech, language and communication delays, but it is important to acknowledge that supporting communication extends beyond simply teaching vocabulary, spoken words or preparing a child for literacy skills. Educators are often engaged in holistic and whole-body ways of communication, and so while it is imperative that we support all aspects of speech, language and communication, this must be in tune with the child's unique development.

What is communication?

Being able to communicate is an important life skill and one which is prioritised in the early years. According to Honig (2007), communication is a social activity based on interactions and a means to share experiences, feelings and activities. Predominantly, we often think of communication as speaking, but it is a holistic concept that includes many components. When thinking of children with SEND, it becomes even more crucial to have a broad understanding of the different ways we might communicate, for example, through non-speaking or motoric actions.

Brodin and Renblad (2019) refer to the idea that children develop a communication identity, and while oral language experiences help children to learn, and should be supported where delays emerge, we should also recognise that for some, communication preferences will always be different. It is useful to have this as a starting point because much of the literature around communication focuses on speech and language delays and the long-term impact, but our approach to reducing the manifestation of such delays isn't always simply about teaching a child to talk; it is about developing a broad range of communicative skills, and more providing opportunities for participation when communication is diverse.

What is language

According to Law et al. (2017), communication begins at birth through innate behaviours such as crying and cooing, and this forms the basis of the infant's interactions with others. Language, by contrast, is a complex symbolic system that develops over time through exposure, use and repetition of that language.

Children's language acquisition is supported by children's daily interactions with trusted others, such as their parents and key people. As soon as babies can babble, adults begin to "pull" language out of them and mould their communication identity through a process known as infant-directed speech. If you observe people around babies, they just can't help but respond to their babbles. It is here that we will often engage in "baby talk," and scientists believe that this reinforces four important skills:

1) Differentiating the sound of words.
2) Matching up tones and words with emotional expressions.
3) Drawing attention to specific words and their meanings.
4) Encouraging the use of language as a form of communication.

This development phase with a young child is fun and exhilarating as reciprocal interactions occur in all sorts of ways, and a child is exposed to sound and language-rich opportunities to communicate.

However, it is important to acknowledge that if a child is D/deaf or has difficulties with infant-directed speech, we can still utilise many different "serve and return" strategies through a process known as whole-body communication. This refers to a range of gestures, behaviours and skills including:

- Verbal communication including speech and talk
- Vocal communication including tone, pace and inflection
- Facial expressions
- Eye gaze and contact

- Body Movement and posture
- Gestures for example pointing, waving and use of body parts to convey and emphasise communication messages

(adapted from Mheidly et al., 2020)

THE ELEMENTS OF LANGUAGE

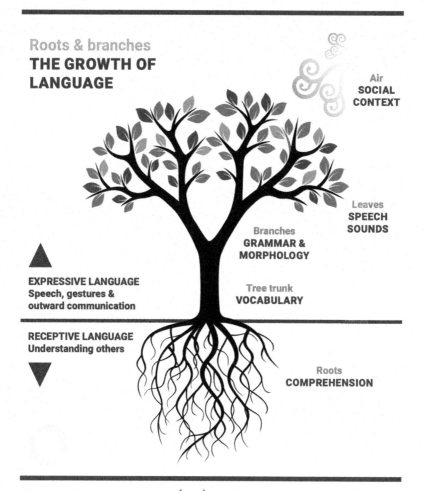

Law, J., Charlton, J., & Asmussen, K. (2017). Child language as a wellbeing indicator.

Speech and language delay

Developing communication skills has an array of benefits for holistic development, including being able to connect with others, communicate needs, express feelings and emotions, and to engage and enhance learning through interactions. Children's development in the early years is fairly rapid, and the desire to communicate starts early as they use all of their kinetic and sensory systems to let us know they are there to be heard and understood. As they grow, so does their capacity for more complex forms of communication, including the use of babble, intonation, body language and words. This is an empowering time for a child, particularly when attempts at communication are reciprocated and needs are met. It is usually in the context of adults that a child's communication begins to thrive and over time, their confidence grows to explore beyond their secure base to interact and "mingle" with peers. Children have an innate desire to connect and communicate through their individual "voice" and if this is not heard or understood, it can become very difficult for a child. Instead of feeling empowered, the child is more likely to feel isolated and may turn to different behaviours to deal with unmet needs. Most educators have experienced a child in distress who, despite all efforts, cannot get their message across. This is often stressful for all involved and often requires some detective skills and a moment of truly listening to the child's personal communication meanings.

Communication needs can, without a doubt, cause barriers to access and participation, and they can stifle other aspects of development. I often say to educators to imagine the exhaustion they may feel if they spent a day having to shout and repeat everything they said ten times over before it was understood, and usually in the case of a child with developmental needs, their absence of key communication skills leads to distressed behaviours that lead to a child being labelled as challenging or difficult to care for. Lack of shared and reciprocal communication can lead to a child feeling frustrated, having greater struggles in forming friendships and more instances of solitary play. This can be particularly challenging when a child's communication identity is likely to be different over a long period of time, and without adequate understanding and support the child becomes further disadvantaged as their needs become greater and more expansive. It is a bleak picture, and one I am often reluctant to write about because I believe that we have become so desensitised to "speech and language stats" that they have become disconnected from the lived experience of the child. Long-term outcomes are associated with anti-social behaviours, criminal futures and unemployment, and while we must recognise the risk of speech, language and communication delays, we must also be aware of the creeping narrative that the child could not be helped or is simply to become just another statistic. We also have to acknowledge that poor outcomes can be the result of a failure to correctly identify a child's needs; for example, does apparent anti-social behaviour occur because of a failure to appropriately diagnose a child early so that they access the right support.

Similarly, we see an ever-increasing emphasis that issues with speech, language and communication needs are rooted in poor parent–child inter-action, exposure to screen technology or deficient parenting. Again, while those factors may indeed play a role, we have to ask how effective are they in encouraging collaborative and respectful partnerships between an edu-cator and a parent, and what shame and stigma are we placing on parents who may use technology or lack confidence in parenting skills. I am not for ignoring, sugar coating or denying the existence of these issues, but from a wellbeing perspective, we always have to be mindful of the narratives that play out in our minds when we spend time with young children.

The language delay "gateway"

When children are very young, it is often difficult to determine the rea-sons underpinning language difficulties. During the early years, language problems are most often apparent when there are delays in a child's ability to meet early language milestones. Hence, the term "language delay" has traditionally been used to describe language problems identified at an early point in children's development, typically before the age of 5. As children grow older, however, language problems become more differentiated; some have difficulties as part of a broader profile of neurodiversity. When thinking about SLCN, always be mindful that the initial concern may be a gateway into an appropriate diagnosis such as autism.

RESEARCH SNIPPETS

It is important that we explore the stories behind the data to avoid taking a deficit approach to SEND support. Consider the following:

- Just 26% of young children with SLCN made expected academic progress in the Early Years Foundation Stage compared with 69% of all children.

  However, keep in mind that the development statements and early learning goals for communication and language are very ableist and focus predominantly on spoken language.

  Think about the holistic ways a child communicates and ensure that this is shared with the Key Stage 1 teacher. It is often those non-speaking forms of communication that provide the scaffolding for speaking.

- 81% of children with emotional and behavioural disorders have unidentified language difficulties, and so we must consider why identification of speech, language and communication needs is still a difficult process.

  This is not helped by the fact that speech and language therapy services are delivering a predominantly universal model amidst funding cuts, and reviews have found that there is a "postcode lottery" of support that disadvantages those most in need. It is also important to establish whether the speech, language and therapy service has a specific understanding of neurodivergence, and that they provide neurodiversity-affirming therapy.

- Children living in areas of social disadvantage are at much higher risk, with around 50% of children starting school with delayed language and other identified SLCN.

  We must be mindful here of not blaming those living within disadvantage and acknowledge that these inequalities are often structural within our society.

  Rather than viewing children as living in poverty, we need to recognise that they are actually living in under-resourced areas, and the way to address that is through adequate funding.

  (Taken from Bercow, 2018)

DID YOU KNOW?

According to Freeman and Kasari (2002), children who engage in play dates with peers outside of their setting have been found to acquire more social and play skills, and to form true friendships. In your setting, do you facilitate playdates between children of different abilities or offer any networking experiences for families to meet and form connects? It is important not to pressure children or families into this, as children should have a genuine connection with each other.

Ways forward

Educators are often faced with significant barriers in SEND support, including timely access to early intervention. There is also an increasing pressure for children to be "school ready" based on a set of goals that do not represent the diversity of children. It can seem that children with SEND are essentially going to fail at the first hurdle for school readiness, and matched with inaccessible therapy, training and support it can feel difficult to know how to move forward. One of the key priorities is to understand the role of adult–child interaction as a foundation for developing communication, followed by an understanding of the diverse pathways that children can develop, and finally, by gaining an understanding of each child's communication identity. With this knowledge, educators can develop a strong pedagogy of teaching and a communication-rich space that is inclusive of all types of communicators.

According to Julie Fisher (2016), interactions are happening consistently within our everyday practice, and are the golden thread of rich learning experiences. Whether this be babbling "conversations" in a baby room, or silly faces pulled between a key person and a toddler, or pointing and modelling as we ask a pre-schooler to follow short instructions. We are constantly in a network of interactions with children, and the spaces which children occupy can provide the thriving foundations for the development of a communication identity.

Communication friendly spaces

According to Curtis and Carter (2014), "spaces are typically created with some kind of purpose or intention, whether or not this is evident. Every environment implies a set of values or beliefs about the people who use a space and the activities that take place there" and so we must consider what our space communicates. When working in an early years environment, whether in a home-based setting or a nursery, we need to consider the ways in which the space supports children with SEND. Early on within my own practice, I became inspired by Elizabeth Jarman's "Communication Friendly Spaces Approach" (2007), which is underpinned by cultivating speaking, listening, emotional wellbeing, physical development and engagement levels. Considering that so many children experience challenges within their speech, language and communication (Bercow, 2019), it is of utmost importance that we plan environments that reduce the risks to this crucial aspect of development.

Get to know before they grow ...

It seems straightforward enough to me that if we "set up" environments too much before we meet children, we are actually hindering our opportunities to develop an inclusive space. If we are neurotypical or non-disabled, then we might lean towards an ableist environment that caters for children whose development takes normative and typical trajectories. While nurseries and childminders often have a steady flow of children throughout the year, there appears to be a summer period in which we have a "spring clean" and we reset. We spend lots of time preparing for transition, but the environment tends to become the forgotten part of those transitions.

Reflection on children owning the space

- Introduce a planning session at the start of September to discuss with children what areas of play they would like, how they think it could work and provide them with cameras to take pictures of their favourite artefacts/areas/toys/resources.
- As a settling-in experience, ask each child (if they are able) to bring in a small item from home (it can be anything) that can live within their nursery environment.
  For example, one nursery I worked with asked each family to donate a "home corner" item, and this then became much more diverse and meaningful to the children's worlds. It also generated lots of language for learning about similarities and differences. The cutlery, for instance, reflected the different cultures within the nursery, including Japanese, English and Indian origin.
- Embrace your own mark-making. Labelling, displays and paper-work should all include handwritten elements, and avoid the overuse of obvious fonts such as comic sans. Our world is print rich and therefore so should children's.
- A good CPD task for this is to ask every member of staff to tally how many different fonts/print they see on their commute to and from work. This opens their thinking that not all displays need the same template.
- Allocate a space for ongoing work by the children, such as an art gallery, or "come back to it table." Provide children with sticky notes so that they can stick it to work they wish to return to, for example, a construction in the block area.
- Send a picture of your early years environment home to a child and family before they start and asked whether they have any feedback on how the space may meet a child's needs? If not, try it. You will find, particularly with SEND parents, that they can often tell you the reasonable adjustments without you having to sit and think them up for yourself.

Noise

Noise can be a difficult aspect of the environment. In some cases, we have educators that want children to be seen and not heard, often introducing absolutely unnecessary "golden rules" that aim to keep children as still and quiet as possible, and then we have the alternative where noise is literally coming through the roof because the sounds of play echo off every single wall. Striking a balance can be challenging particularly because many early years spaces are not purpose-built. It is important to acknowledge that noise is good, especially if it consists of highly engaged and involved children, but the space needs to account for several volume buttons. Children need spaces to react, retreat and relax.

Light

Discussions on lighting come up a lot when thinking about wellbeing. Educators shared the following with me:

EDUCATOR'S VOICE

My nursery became obsessed with fairy lights; they were everywhere. Even the activities had fairy lights dotted around them. My key child would not go near activities that would otherwise have been really beneficial for her key skills. I didn't want to say anything because I felt like we were being difficult criticising the set-up of an activity.

EDUCATOR'S VOICE

My key child was having significant meltdowns towards the end of every day. It turned out it was the impact of the constant glare of the strip lighting. He was completely unable to communicate the tired-ness, dehydration and headaches caused by artificial light.

DID YOU KNOW?

Research has found that fluorescent bulbs can contribute to anxiety, poor attention, hyperactivity and depression (Martell, 1992). While it is also said that natural sunlight is best for our development (Heschong et al., 2002), it is important to acknowledge that often the issue with light and sensory processing is the glare, flicker and buzz. For example, a glare from a lamp or bright sun can be equally disruptive to a child with SEND. I make this point because we seem to have ventured towards aesthetic lighting over conducive to learning lighting. Switching all the "big lights" off and recreating IKEA's lamp station in your environment is not the answer to inclusive spaces. The lamp may still flicker, and the fairy lights may buzz. Try not to prescribe to one form of lighting. It might change according to needs. It might be that at different points in the day, you require different forms of lighting, or reasonable adjustments need to be made for individual needs.

 # Wellbeing strategy

Scaffolding language and communication

One of the most common strategies that is used in speech, language and communication is scaffolding. This strategy is usually already in an educators "toolkit," but its importance can be overlooked as something that just happens naturally. We should be intentional in our scaffolding and use "teachable moments" to build up both spoken language and broader communication. Let's consider some examples:

+One

The child may say a singular word, for example, "car," and the educator will add a word, for example, "red car." Or a child may use an action sign, and you can add a sign or action back.

Correct yourself, not the child

A child may utter a word but without the correct pronunciation. Never correct the child but repeat back with the correct word. For example, a child says "boc," and you say "yes, the bottle." This same technique works for developing accurate signing actions.

Back it up

When a child is building up their understanding and communication, ensure that you back up what you say with body language, objects of reference.

Start it off ...

A useful way to kickstart language is to use sentence starters, with open-ended aspects, for example, "When we go outside today, we could ...?." The key here is not to put pressure on children for an answer but to ask in a pondering way so that the child has space to think and respond. Remember that this strategy can also be used with non-speaking children, and you use a "sentence strip" with visuals and recognise non-speaking action responses. For example, a child may understand what you have asked, and may point or move to indicate their intentions. Value all communication.

Mirror and model

It is very common to hear the modelling strategy used in the early years, but I often encourage educators to first start with mirroring. The whole premise of "meeting the child where they are" means that we actually should be mirroring what they do to develop some idea of their perspective. I also find this starting point much more respectful of a child's play, and it demonstrates that we value what they do in their everyday play, behaviour and actions.

Play pauses

Play is diverse and multi-modal, and when a child is beginning to build confidence through their play, it is important they have time to process and experiment with different ways of playing. While we are modelling, an important skill is to use play pauses so that the child has time to observe the different way a resource can be played with.

Visuals

Visuals are crucial for supporting children with SEND, especially those who may have communication, cognition or processing difficulties. As a setting, it is important to identify a consistent set of visuals, and to differentiate according to the child's needs. For some children, this may include a specific visual structure, whereas other children might need prompts. Visuals are supportive because:

- They are permanent.
  The permanence of a visual means a child can use it to hold information in mind. Spoken words can be hard to process, and communication can move on quite quickly.
- They increase independence.
  as children become confident with visuals, they can become more independent, and initiate tasks and communication.
- Reduce anxiety.
  visuals can take the pressure off a child having to consume lots of information and language. They help a child to navigate communication safely.
- They enhance and support other forms of communication.
  Contrary to belief, using visuals or signs does not limit communication but enhances it building up opportunities to experiment more freely with communication, and to build confidence in being playful with communication.
- They help with change and transitions.
  Visuals can be used to support a child with change and transitions and serve as reminders and prompts. They can also be used to support a child to work through the sequences of change, for example, going to wash hands before snack.

- They can be transferred.
  If used consistently, visuals can be transferred to different settings and can expand.
- They don't have a tone.
  It can sometimes be difficult for a child to sense the tone, and visuals do not come with this issue as they can be adapted to suit the needs of the child.

Dependent on the child's communication style, you can utilise visuals in different ways, but remember that for some children, too much visual information can in itself be overwhelming. It is best to speak with a specialist to agree on the best forms of visuals to access:

Objects of reference	Photograph	Colour picture	Colour symbol	Line drawing	Written words
Some children will respond well to objects of reference used alongside spoken language.	Settings may adopt the use of visual routines with photographs.	Colour pictures can be used alongside written words to provide key information to children.	The colour symbol can be utilised in visual routines, now and next boards and schedules.	For some children, busy visuals can cause confusion, and sometimes line drawings are more appropriate to clearly convey a word or meaning.	Written words can be used alongside the visuals, and support children's literacy skills.

OREO

Observe

As observers, we should be developing the "tuning-in-zooming-in" skill of observation. We look closely for signs of learning, signals for interaction and play behaviours. We aren't observing to simply write something down on a sticky note. Instead, view yourself as a detective who is investigating what you see.

You are determining what the play indicates and whether you are welcome to engage. A concern always in play is that an educator will interrupt and interfere where support is actually not needed.

Respond

We often think "respond" means to interact, but oftentimes our response is to choose not to interact as we can see self-directed or peer-mediated learning. Alternatively, you may spot a need to scaffold or guide the learning.

Engage

You may pose a question, provide a commentary, offer a possibility or solution, ponder or offer to model and demonstrate.

You may do this in a direct ("you could play this block here") or indirect way ("I think I will have a go").

Observe

The educator can remove support and return to observation.

OREO communicates many things to a child:

1) My key person is there for me if I need them.
2) My key person isn't here to take me away from my play.
3) My key person trusts me.
4) My key person believes in me.
5) My key person respects my play.
   - You continue to "tune-in and zoom-in," but you are transient in your play facilitation. Julie Fisher, author of "Interfering or Interacting," often refers to this as choosing whether to "meddle in the middle."
   - This series of good-fit interactions increase children's independence within play, and research suggests that this leads to self-regulation skills with increased opportunity for inquiry-based play, including mathematical competencies.
   - This model also works with children with developmental differences who may need scaffolding but are still very much agenda-driven.

- Good-fit interactions lead to children engaging in more complex types of play. They will take risks, test out ideas, self-regulate and show increasing confidence and competency in key emergent academic skills.
- Poor-fit interactions lead to children engaging in surface-level play, and their ideas do not elaborate beyond the basics. They feel stifled by the constant interruption and re-direction. They begin to see fewer possibilities.

(Adapted from Trawick-Smith and Dzuirgot, 2010)

 RESEARCH SNIPPETS

Research suggests that communication is best cultivated in play situations. This is quite intriguing considering many intervention programmes that focus on SLCN take children away from play and promote more structured approaches that focus on whole body listening and attention skills as a foundation for language and communication. Think about the following pieces of research. How do you support SEND and communication in your spaces?

- Generally children speak more words and complex sentences when they are playing (Cohen and Uhry, 2007).
- Children with a variety of disabilities, including Autism speak (communicate) more often and show their most advanced forms of language when they play (Chang et al., 2018).
- Play allows for private speech, communication and self-regulation; for example, pretend play has been found to support the development of self-regulation skills (Berk and Meyers, 2013) as children can engage in private speech, which supports them to process their emotional experiences.

Video modelling

Video modelling is a way to teach new skills or behaviours to autistic children but can be utilised more broadly. Video modelling was first used for an autistic child in 1982 by researchers Monika Steinborn and Terry J. Knapp. They used videos of local streets to teach the child pedestrian skills. The video shows someone doing a skill or behaviour, and the child watching the video then practises copying the behaviour. It is important to be mindful that we take account of a child's differences when using video modelling, and we should ensure that we include examples of their own ways of doing things. It is not to be used to teach children neurotypical skills.

There are four types of video modelling:

- Basic video modelling: this uses other adults, peers or animation as models.
- Video self-modelling: this uses the autistic child as the model.
- Point of view video modelling: this shows what completing the task would look like from the child's point of view. For example, the video shows a pair of hands doing a task.
- Video-prompting: this breaks up a task like brushing teeth into steps that the child watches as they complete the task.

Attention grabbers

You might often find that simply calling a child's name or trying to gain and engage their attention can be difficult. The use of attention grabbers can be useful as an additional way to gain attention. This strategy is relatively straightforward and involves novel items that would pique curiosity. Explore some of the examples below:

- During transition points, use a brightly coloured resource that either lights up or makes sound so that the child looks over, and then you can provide an instruction or information.
- During group activities, use a novel item to draw children's eyes to different things, such as follow the magic wand.
- Complete short burst activities to build attention, for example, presenting a wind-up toy and encouraging the children to watch.

Pause for thought

In a busy early years environment, it is very common to end up giving lots of instructions and having quite high expectations for children to respond in a "timely manner." When I spend time in early years settings, I often end up advising that they press the pause button much more often and generally slow the pace of things down. There is often a real sense of urgency in early years spaces, and this pressure on both the staff and children can be too much. Using pauses, including extending wait times when providing instructions or asking questions can make a lot of difference to the daily atmosphere and children being able to engage in task completion.

Lots of educators have heard of the ten-second rule, but it really does depend on the context of the child. A strategy I have recently been trying with educators is "the pause for thought" technique, and it goes like this:

Call child's name
Pause for thought – one mindful breath
Give and model instruction part 1
Pause for thought – one mindful breath
Pause for praise – acknowledge the success of the action
Give and model instruction part 2
Pause for through – one mindful breath
Pause for praise – acknowledge the success
And continue until task completion.

This method is useful because it takes the pressure off everyone. Slowing our pace means that children do not feel under pressure to perform and can learn to do things fully present.

Objects of reference

Objects of reference are objects used to represent a person, activity or event. Over time the person learns that the object stands for that person, activity or event. Objects of reference are used to help a person understand what is happening in their environment and also be used to help people make choices.

Chatter spaces

Research has found that children are often more likely to experiment with more complex language when in spaces that are not overly occupied by adults. This is often referred to as a private speech and allows a child to engage with language in a stress-free state. Look around your early year's environment and think whether there are places where children can engage in this type of chatter. Think creatively about the ways in which you can create more privacy.

Fidgets and fiddles

The environment will benefit from items that children can fidget and fiddle with. This often helps children to maintain attention and can help with focus. Fidget boxes can be dotted around the space and children can independently access them when they feel they need to be doing something with their hands.

Say my name and tone of voice

Have you ever been in a situation where someone has asked you something but not used your name, and it has taken a few moments for your mind to process? Often, it can be the little things that make the difference, so if we are communicating with a child, it is important we use their name. Also, think about the intonation you use when speaking to a child, do we always use their name in a particular way, for example, with a child who may not always appear to be listening, do we more often say their name in a negative intonation. Think about the impact this might have on a child's self-esteem

Play scripts

One way to support a child with entry into play with peers and engagement in pretend and role-play is to use play scripts. In our usual everyday practice, we wouldn't necessarily dictate to a child what they should say or roles they could play, but for children with SEND it can sometimes be beneficial to give them the tools of pretend play through scripts. Trawick-Smith provides the following example:

> An educator and autistic child head over to the role-play area together where the children are playing, and suggests "why don't we be the post people." She hands the child some envelopes, and they approach the front door; the educator suggests, "You can say 'hey children, here are your letters'" and the child repeats. It is at this moment that the educator can be provided feedback and encouragement.
>
> (Adapted 2018)

Strategies to avoid

Do not force eye contact

It is not uncommon for educators to become quite fixated on the fact that some children struggle to provide and maintain eye contact. It is usually also one of the common descriptors given when sharing concerns about a child's development, and the possibility of the child being autistic. First, it is important to consider that eye contact is quite an intimate social form of communication, and you might remember the days as a child completing starting contests to see who would blink first, or who would have to look away because it all felt too much. There are many reasons why a child or adult may struggle with eye contact, such as feeling overwhelmed, being distracted, feeling under pressure or being sensory overloaded, and it is important that we do not place too much emphasis on correcting this behaviour. By demanding eye contact, we likely make the experience and ability much harder to develop. The focus should instead be on developing joint attention. One such way is to use objects for eye tracking. For example, if you are playing alongside a child, you may pick up an item, and place it near your face for a brief moment of connection, and then redirect (Charlop, Lang and Rispoli, 2018).

SEND friendly spaces

Does the environment make sense?

- The environment makes sense and communicates key messages to the child; for example, there are signposts and labels.
- Their layout is designed so that children can choose to be in low arousal or high arousal spaces, in which they can navigate their preferred style of communication.
- The environment does not feel restrictive and contained.
- There is adequate access to outdoor spaces.

All forms of communication are welcomed

- There are quiet hideaway spaces for private speech.
- The layout encourages small chatter between peers and adult–child.
- The environment does not feel restrictive and contained.
- There is adequate access to outdoor spaces.
- Children are not only encouraged to use their "quiet voices" but are given opportunities to develop their intonation, and to use their sounds and voice to express emotion.
- Approaches to facilitate an alternative form of communication, e.g. use of signs (Makaton) and symbols/pictorial labels will be used as appropriate.
- Adults use language at the right level for the child's stage of development.
- Children with language and communication needs are given frequent opportunities to participate, by any means possible, e.g. using objects, gestures, pictures and/or words.
- Visual supports, such as visual timetables, props, story bags, song/rhyme bags etc., are used to support children's communication.
- Ensure that the use of visual supports is consistent. Do not mix up visual timetables or use symbols from different programmes.
- Use personal communication dictionaries to ensure that natural gesture and communication is recorded and understood.
- Ensure that programmes such as Makaton are used consistently, and that all children are taught signs and actions.
- Adults get down to the children's level when interacting with them.
- Adults ask genuine questions that extend children's thinking, but don't bombard them with unnecessary questions.
- Adults give children plenty of time to respond and take turns in interacting with them.
- Educators can describe children's communication skills and needs accurately.

Conclusion

When supporting speech, language and communication needs, we must consider a child's holistic communication identity. There can be a tendency for educators to favour speaking over all other skills, but children with developmental differences may have diverse communication preferences, for example, through movement or visual prompts.

Children will work very hard to be understood, and at times this may be demonstrated through a range of behaviours. We may need to work harder to figure things out and connect with the child's personal meanings, but by doing so, we support the child's unique "voice" to be heard. When children feel heard and understood, we can better meet their wants and needs and provide communication friendly spaces that help them to thrive. Embracing all forms of communication means that we provide spaces that promote a child's wellbeing to feel safe and secure enough to fully participate in their early years experiences.

 Read, watch and listen

The Communication Trust (Early Years)
http://www.thecommunicationtrust.org.uk/early-years/

Bercow Ten Years on Report
https://www.bercow10yearson.com/

ICAN Early Years Educator Guidance
https://ican.org.uk/i-cans-talking-point/professionals/early-years
-educators/

6 | Cognition and learning needs

Defining cognition and learning

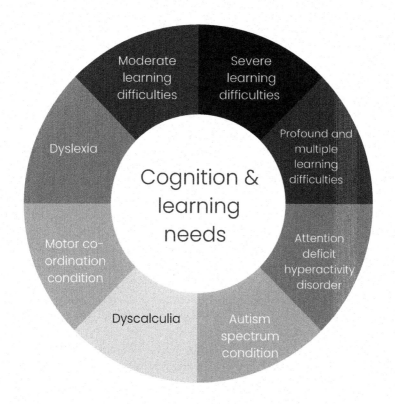

DOI: 10.4324/9781003138365-6

Cognition refers to the thinking skills and thought processes that a child has acquired through development, experience and learning. Learning needs are on a continuum and can vary across skills and situations. Children with learning difficulties may learn at a slower pace than their peers despite appropriate differentiation. Learning difficulties can be general or specific. Specific learning difficulties (SpLD) affect one or more specific aspects of learning. This encompasses a range of conditions such as dyslexia, dyscalculia and dyspraxia. Difficulties are often described as mild, moderate, severe or profound, and are usually underpinned by genetic and biological factors. Educators should be mindful that the degree of difficulty may differ and change over time, and with any disability, cognition and learning difficulties include strengths and diverse profiles.

Defining profound and multiple learning difficulties

- Children with profound and multiple learning difficulties fall under the category of complex needs.
- Children may have severe learning difficulties and differences along with physical disabilities, sensory needs or a medical condition.
- Children with PMLD will often require a high level of adult support, and the educational setting will need to have a strong underpinning knowledge of their needs with accessible specialist provision, support and expertise.
- Children with PMLD will have needs beyond their learning, including dignity, personal care and social and emotional support.
- Alternative and augmentative communication profiles will be likely and may consist of basic or complex ways of connecting with others.

Individualised and specialist support is often in place for children with complex needs, and in this chapter, we will consider general and cognition and learning differences and difficulties.

All disabilities consist of strengths, traits, symptoms and difficulties. According to Imray and Colley (2017), there may be symptoms or difficulties that require ongoing support, and specific adaptations that are informed by specialists. The key to acknowledging this, however, is not to situate the child in a position of weakness or dependency but to explore the levels of support they will need, to identify what they can do, and to decide on long-term needs and adaptations.

STARTING POINTS

When observing practice in a local preschool, I noticed that the space was quite busy and chaotic. There were lots of instructions being given to children, and there was an expectation to do tasks that perhaps adults might also find difficult. This was clearly overwhelming to the children. In one instance, the educator called over to a child and asked him to complete a sequence of instructions. The child appeared to freeze, clearly confronted by the wave of information. The educator became impatient emphasising her instruction again in the exact same way. The child grasped to understand the wave of information but became even more overwhelmed. The educator then simply said, "you never do as you are told," and walked off.

What is your initial reflection of this moment?
How might it feel for the child?
What challenges might the child be facing at this moment?
How could this child be appropriately supported to follow instructions?

Introduction

In the previous chapters, I covered the key domains of child development and considered how these interconnect with and become springboards for thinking and learning. For example, for children to learn, they need to be able to feel safe and secure, have opportunities for movement and exploration, and they need to be able to communicate their needs. With these solid foundations, children are then able to organise their thinking in order to learn. Over time, children develop individual learning characteristics, and through their play, they demonstrate engagement, motivation and critical thinking skills. While, in many cases, the tools of the EYFS (DfE, 2021) help us to understand a good majority of children, sometimes we require additional guidance to really tune-into the unique needs of each child. The types of neurodivergent and disability needs can be complex for us to understand, especially where a child has profound or multiple learning difficulties. So, an understanding of brain development and key cognitive processes such as executive function can be useful in ensuring that we provide a 'brain compatible' learning experience.

Brain Buzzwords

Neuroscience

In recent years, there has been an explosion of interest in brain development during the early years. Neuroscience, which is the scientific study of the brain and human nervous system, has enabled a greater exploration of brain architecture including key processes which influence child development. For example, according to Harvard University's Centre on the Developing Child, infants will seek connection with a caregiver through interactions such as babble, gesture and facial expressions and they will look for a connecting response. This is often referred to as "serve and return" and has been found to help build the strong architectural foundations in the brain which supports later learning. This type of knowledge helps us to become better practitioners because we can act upon this knowledge to be responsive to children's initiations for connection. However, our understanding of how the brain works is still within its infancy. In *How Children Learn* (2020), Rodd explains that we should remain vigilant that neuroscience does not currently hold all the answers we seek. For example, the exact cause of many neurodevelopmental profiles such as autism remains unknown, and many factors are considered to be at play. We should be informed yet active in ensuring that we do not misinterpret or poorly apply research findings into practice. This is equally important when we think about developmental differences and delays because outdated research can often influence practice in harmful ways. For example, Professor Simon Baron Cohen's studies of Theory of Mind (ToM) which is the ability to understand the mental states of others has long influenced the "no empathy" stereotype applied to autistic people. This claim has been debunked and criticised for a myriad of reasons, yet the societal harm of this view lives on (Gernsbacher and Yergeau, 2019) and dominates our knowledge and practice. There is increasing evidence of the double empathy theory which states that knowing how the brain works and how we can become neuro-informed is a wonderful thing, but it is dependent on our ability to question how robust the research might be.

Neuromyths

TRUE OR FALSE?

Read the following scientific statements about neuroscience. Which do you believe to be true, and which do you believe to be false (answers revealed on page 199)?

- We only use 10% of our brain.
- Individuals learn better when they receive information in their preferred learning style (e.g. auditory, visual, kinaesthetic).
- Differences in hemispheric dominance (left brain, right brain) can help explain individual differences among learners.
- Children are less attentive after consuming sugary drinks and/or snacks.
- Learning problems associated with developmental differences in brain function cannot be remediated by education.
- A common sign of dyslexia is seeing letters backwards.
- Listening to classical music increases children's reasoning ability.
- Everything that is important for brain development occurs within the first three years.
- Following a specific diet can help overcome certain neurological disabilities, such as ADHD, dyslexia and autism spectrum conditions.
- Doing basic Brain Gym exercises help students to learn to read and use language better.

(adapted from Torrijos-Muelas et al., 2021)

Over the past decade, there has been a significant merging of our understanding of the brain and neuroscience within education, often referred to as "neuroeducation," but there has also been an increase in neuromyths.

A neuromyth has been described as "a misconception generated by a misunderstanding, a misreading, or a misquoting of facts scientifically established (by brain research) to make a case for the use of brain research in education and other contexts" (OECD, 2002).

- Why might neuromyths be harmful in our practice?
- Are there any neuromyths that have you prescribed to and cited?
- How can we ensure that we check our facts?

Survey studies have found that beliefs in neuromyths are remarkably prevalent, and efforts to reduce these beliefs have been effective but haven't fully eliminated the issue. A significant concern is that even those who have taken part in neuroscience training endorse many of the myths (46%), and over half of the educators surveyed believed in neuromyths (65%) Macdonald et al, 2017). Another factor to consider is that many neuromyths relate to special educational needs and disabilities. It is, therefore, crucial that we do not become too attached to neuro-informed strategies that hold little true value in practice. What we do know about the brain is that in early childhood, it is expanding at an incredible rate, and neurons are overproduced to to help a child navigate early life. By the time a child reaches age 5, their brain has made billions of connections which forms the foundational architecture (Rushton, 2011). So, for anyone in the presence of children, you can play a significant role in providing meaningful experiences, and to help organise and mould those early thinking (cognitive) and learning skills.

Cognition and Executive Function

Before we explore executive function, it is important to highlight that children can sometimes be described according to their level of functioning, for example, low and high-functioning autism. This is problematic because it suggests that autism is on a linear spectrum and that there is a preferable type of autism. Functioning labels are unhelpful because they do not account for the fact that our ability to function from day-to-day is influenced by many different factors. Our role is not to make a fixed judgement on a child's ability to function, but to make the relevant adaptations to support them to thrive.

Cognition in its simplest form means thinking, and researchers commonly explore this through executive functions. According to Miyake and Friedman (2017), executive function (EF) is the umbrella term used to characterise a set of thinking processes that guide our everyday functioning and goal-directed behaviours (Fuster, 2008). While there is no definitive consensus on the definition of EF, it has been described as "the ability to hold in mind information in working memory, to inhibit fast and unthinking responses to stimulation, and to flexibly shift the focus of one's mental frame" (Blair, 2016). Executive functions enable individuals to act in self-directed ways and control their behaviours, for example, by managing their impulses and regulating their emotions (Scionti et al., 2020). In other words, our executive function provides the conditions so that we can learn. For example, imagine not being able to recall information, or to remember the instructions you are given. These everyday skills are often things we take for granted, especially if we consider ourselves to be able to do them well, but the truth is that executive function is not a "one size fits all" model. There are many factors that can enhance or disrupt our executive function skills. Functioning skills can differ from day to day, or there may be a specific area in which a child needs support or adaptations. When a child's needs are not understood, it can make access to participation and learning very difficult, and so we must be flexible to the neurodiversity and neurodivergence of executive function.

Executive function skills emerge in early childhood and continue to develop across the lifespan contributing to social and academic outcomes (Lopez et al., 2017; Blair and Raver, 2015). EF plays an important role in multiple areas of child development, such as social cognition, communicative behaviour and behaviour (Moriguchi et al., 2008, 2010). Research has found that the development of executive function also helps children in their readiness for learning, and the skills of memory, attention and emotional self-regulation positively predict literacy, vocabulary and math skills as early as the end of the preschool years (McClelland et al., 2007; Welsh et al., 2010)

Research continues to identify that although executive function appears to develop over a long period the window of opportunity and most impressive change is during the preschool period (Garon et al., 2008), and such skills provide the architecture for more formal learning (Friedman and Miyake, 2004). From an educational viewpoint, executive function development occurs through consistent relationships, high-quality interactions, scaffolding, play and from being in low stress environments. On the contrary, high stress and adult-directed expectations, including being expected to sit for long periods can disrupt executive function (Rosas et al., 2019).

Below is a table of what executive function skills look like in our everyday actions:

Skill	Definition	Support
Working memory	*Holding information in mind, and being able to retain, recall and act upon that information.*	• Provide enjoyable and self-directed repetitive experiences • Slow the pace of instructions • Break information down into sequences and bitesize information • Be patient and introduce short waiting times between providing information. • Provide visuals, prompts and reminders
Flexible thinking	*Tolerating and adapting to change and transitions. Unexpected events do not activate too much stress.*	• Reminders and cues between changes and transitions. • Providing clear information and instructions. • Making use of visuals and prompts. • Rehearse possibilities. • Using social stories. • Co-regulation through mirroring and modelling key behaviours.
Impulse control	*Being able to think things through before acting and having control over physical and emotional actions.*	• Providing sensory breaks. • Using visual risk assessments and prompts to support with understanding impulses. • Providing "react" resources such as fidgets or heavy work items.
Emotional control	*Being able to identify or feel familiar with feelings, to sit with them and keep them in-sync.*	• Use RULER steps when a child is distressed (see page 63). • Provide choice during co-regulation. • Naming and labelling feelings. • Using stories to explore emotions.Do not distract, but allow time to spend feeling feelings

(Continued)

(Continued)

Skill	Definition	Support
Self-direction	Being able to monitor and direct oneself independently. Child is motivated, engaged and works towards goals in their play.	• Introducing choice boards based on the child's favourite things to do. • Uninterrupted child-led play. • Planning for interests, including special and intense interests often common in neurodivergence such as autism and ADHD. • Having high-quality continuous provision. • Backwards chaining (see page 151). • Scaffolding during play. • Using social stories and visual sequences of play skills and resources. • Use engagement scales with the child, for example, likes and dislikes chart.
Planning and prioritising	Being able to engage in play and to sustain attention, make plans and keeping on track.	• Providing images of play at different stages. • Using video observations to look back at play. • Introduce a "come back to it" strategy. • Break tasks down into manageable chunks. • Valuing the child's priorities wherever possible. • Provide extra time to complete play, tasks and routines.
Task initiation	Being able to initiate an activity or play in own way and know how things work.	• Mirror the child's play, followed by modelling. • Introduce provocations, discovery baskets and the toy box. • Follow the child's lead and introduce motivators in play.
Organisation	Being able to keep track of things physically, emotionally and cognitively.	• Use play mats to demarcate play spaces. • Clearly label and signpost resources. • Use the environment as a third teacher. • Use visual prompts and routines. • Provide repetitive experiences.

Imagine if a child had difficulty in any of the above areas, how might the wellbeing scales be tipped?

 PLAYING, LEARNING AND THINKING

Have you ever said?

"All he does is line things up."
"He never joins in."
"He flits between different areas with no purpose."
"How is she going to cope when she goes to school?"
"All she does is run around."

As you can imagine, if we exist within a sector that focuses predominantly on a child's impairments, it will become commonplace to overlook all the uniquely diverse ways children learn and to build upon these. There tends to be an issue that once educators are aware of a child's SEND, they stop seeing them as learners, but rather a set of problems to be fixed. Additionally, educators are placed under pressure to help children with SEND to catch up, and so the focus becomes more about closing gaps than deeply understanding children. Learning opportunities are also often missed because the behaviours we observe simply become symptoms related to their specific condition or disability, for example, deciding that a lining things up is a symptom of autism rather than a play trait of autism. The above statements are taken from discussions I have had with educators who have categorised all behaviours as SEND rather than potential learning behaviours or unique forms of play.

In my previous book, *A Guide to SEND in the Early Years* (2021), I wrote extensively about the idea that play is denied to neurodivergent and disabled children. After all, we assume they cannot play because our definition of play is generally relatively narrow and written through an ableist lens. As educators, we have to expand our ideas of play and disabilities, and continue to challenge resources, tools and descriptions that only describe the typically developing child. We need to push back on continually creating things in addition to, or separate from mainstream documentation, which continue to push the narrative of marginalisation and segregation. We must accept that *all* children engage in play, and as Jeffrey Trawick-Smith (2019) correctly points out, "there is no optimal way to play." This is not to say that children do not need support to play, but play is inherent within every child. Intrinsic to the issue of play denial, is the idea of a play-based provision, because this simply does not describe the reality of the early years, and as a sector we should be aiming for play richness which is inclusive of all children. In recent years, I prescribe to the idea that we should be aiming towards richness because of the benefits this has for learning and wellbeing. An inclusive play-rich curriculum consists of the following principles:

- Inclusive play-rich provision is child-centred and child-led.
- The early years environment belongs to the child and is informed by the child.
- The provision is considered a foundation and springboard for creating a safe, secure and contented learning environment for promoting independence.
- The practice revolves around understanding how children play and learn, not just what they learn, taking into account lifelong skills and characteristics of effective learning.
- Children's strengths, interests, differences and needs are all welcomed and understood in the context of the holistic child.
- The provision is differentiated, scaffolded and facilitated by play partners and play protagonists.
- It promotes security, safe risk, scaffolding up and self-direction.

Play is the foundation for all learning, and as educators, no matter what decisions we are making for children with SEND, they should be rooted in play accessibility, and developing an understanding of what play might look like for that particular child. Unfortunately, this will require you to go beyond the non-statutory documents we have such as the "Development Matters" and "Birth to Five Matters" because they are quite exclusionary to SEND learners, especially those with complex learning needs and so there are efforts required to break down our current understanding of play and development, and to critically explore the finer components of play. Play is also the gateway for us to understand a child's development, and to consider their unique blueprint for learning. For this, we are often guided by curriculum frameworks, and child development documents, but we have to consider whether we see all children within these documents.

The characteristics of effective learning and the continuum of engagement

When working with children with SEND, we can sometimes overlook aspects of the EYFS because we might assume that the child will not "fit in" to those aspects, but it is important that with all children we first consider how they learn before what they learn. The characteristics of effective learning of engagement, motivation, and critical thinking (DfE, 2021) are a good starting point to really explore the learning profile of a child with SEND. For some children, however, the characteristics of effective learning may not best describe the child, particularly when a child has complex needs. It is always important to think about how we can deconstruct some of these approaches so that they are inclusive of children who have a range of engagement and learning approaches. Education Scotland uses a tool which breaks down learning and engagement into more specific statements. This means that those with complex development needs can be more accurately understood:

Experiences	Encounters	Learner is present during an activity or experience
	Notices	Learner appears to be aware of what is happening around them.
	Shows interest	Learner demonstrates some interest in people, events or objects
Actively engages	Responds	Learner attends and begins to give reactions to show that he/she can tell the difference between people, events or objects
	Focuses attention	Learner demonstrates more consistent attention and shows a clear distinction between specific people, events or objects
	Participates actively	Learner begins to be proactive in their interactions with people, events and objects. He/she anticipates familiar sequence of events
	Initiates	Learner initiates activities and interactions more regularly and responds to options and choices
Applies and extends	Demonstrates understanding	Learner demonstrates their understanding and skills in a specific learning setting
	Consolidates	Learner recalls previous learning and can use it in familiar situations.
	Extends	Learner becomes more confident in their learning and can apply skills in a range of unfamiliar settings.

Source: Education Scotland Milestones to support learners with complex additional support needs (2019)

Settings might also break down development into smaller steps for children with SEND. This is a great way to ensure that we can offer the appropriate scaffolding for learning, but we must be mindful that we don't see these documents as holding less importance or value than the normative "milestones" and statements. We should also be mindful of infantalising children's development. For example, using age bands to describe children can lead to us suggesting neurodivergent or disabled children are learning lower than their age, rather than having a different developmental profile. I often explain to educators that these documents deconstruct development so that we can reinterpret it for a child with SEND. By doing this there are greater opportunities to expand our ideas of diverse learning and development, and to become more inclusive.

One of the most important vehicles for learning is through play and using a play lens to make sense of children's cognitive processes is invaluable.

Intervention integration

Often children are talked about as though they need to be integrated into the mainstream environment, but it is actually the intervention strategies and

approaches that require integration. I spoke with an educational psychologist who explained the following:

> The way to view an intervention programme is that it provides a structured
> model or framework for supporting a child's specific needs and this will even-
> tually be translated into the child's everyday experiences. The intervention pro-
> gramme is not the whole story. The thing educators need to consider is that
> intervention programmes may improve a child's skills or learning in a particular
> area, but the length of time those skills remain can differ. Researchers specifi-
> cally study this idea of looking at the after-effects of an intervention (how long
> it lasts). What researchers are depending on is that the adult learns new teach-
> ing habits and skills that filter into everyday practice based on that intervention.
> And it is this that likely makes the difference. If you are looking for your "cure"
> in an intervention programme, you will not get it.

Additionally, research has found that children respond best in their naturalistic
spaces, including the home and early years setting, and so time should be spent
integrating interventions rather than seeing them as a separate entity. During a
training session, I demonstrated this idea to a group of educators. What stood
out is that the educators were already carrying out lots of high-quality teaching
practices, but they were doing this without clear intention. When we become
intentional in what we do, we begin to see more clearly the impact we can
have on children's development, and this is where reflection occurs:

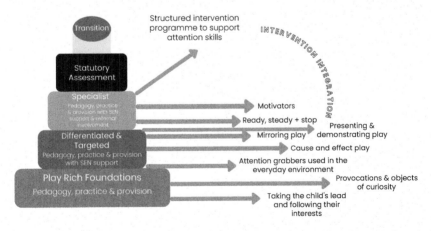

If you look at the above image, you will see that in the specialist section, the setting may choose to use a specific intervention programme but they should think about how these skills are integrated into everyday practice, for example, the use of attention grabbers in the environment or presenting activities and including novel aspects. This will also be matched with general everyday teaching strategies and techniques, and so overall, the child's SEND is not viewed in isolation from their play or everyday experiences.

Participation in learning

According to a report by the European Commission, for children to actively engage in their learning, educators should consider the following:

- Children should have full participation in all activities, and experiences and this includes reasonable adjustments and careful consideration of how inclusive provision is.
- Cultivating friendships between children with a recognition that understanding differences are "part and parcel" of the social dynamic. Educators should not deny the existence of difference in front of children, for example, stating that all children are the same, when they are not.
- Reinforcing the behaviours that will help them to engage effectively, for example, providing meaningful praise and feedback, having routines and rhythms for a sense of structure and familiarity and not focus too much on "correcting" behaviours.
- Using assistive technology and support to ensure that children's holistic development is accounted for, for example, the use of visuals to support understanding of a task, or examples of how something can be played with.

Wellbeing strategies

Types of support

According to Education Scotland, there are a number of ways in which we can support children with PMLD through our everyday actions and provision.

- Physical supports, for example, hand-under-hand or adaptive equipment.
- Gestural supports including simple signs, gestures, pointing and demonstrating.
- Visual support including the use of objects, photos, pictures and symbols.
- Verbal support such as prompting, cues, encouragement, pauses and intensive interaction.
- Support via technology such as apps and communication aids.

If there is a child within the setting that has complex needs, it is useful to use these types of support as a starting point for building a learning profile. Educators will often feel anxious when a child had complex or multiple needs, but upon further exploration, we can see that having these basic aspects are often accessible, and within our toolkit of teaching behaviours already.

Scaffolding specific skills

When supporting a child who may have cognitive and learning difficulties, it is important to scaffold support when teaching key skills. Keep the following in mind:

- Be as concrete as possible by providing a verbal cue, a visual cue (image, symbol, or photograph or environmental support), and a tactile cue (model the action).
- Reflection: think about the task of handwashing before eating. What verbal, visual and tactile cues could you provide?
- Break down tasks into smaller steps, so you know what to expect and can therefore appropriately support the child.
- Give all kinds of feedback so that when a child is working through a sequence, they know they are on the right track. By all kinds of feedback, this includes facial expression, words, actions such as a thumbs up, nodding and encouragement. Acknowledging the smaller steps will help the child build up to task completion.

- Forward's chaining means to start teaching the child the first step in a sequence of actions, for example, focusing on doing one button on their coat and building up so they can do all buttons. You can also use backwards chaining for this, as highlighted below.

 BACKWARDS CHAINING

Case study

Hattie is 4 years old and loves dance and music. She is an active child despite having physical development needs. More recently, Hattie has become upset because she isn't always able to complete tasks at the same pace as her peers. For example, fastening up the buttons on her coat can be difficult as she struggles with fine motor control. She is noticing her differences and is aware that an adult often has to do things for her. The setting is keen to develop strategies that give Hattie a sense of accomplishment. Her key person decided to use the "backwards chaining" strategy during everyday tasks. This task involves the adult supporting the first set of steps in a task, and Hattie completes the last step in the sequence so that she is engaged in accomplishing a task and is building the occupational skills. The key person fastens the first four buttons on the jacket, and Hattie fastens the last. Using this strategy instead of merely doing these tasks on behalf of Hattie provides opportunities for feedback, praise and encouragement. It also makes the task less daunting. Her key person has noticed that Hattie shows pride in fastening the buttons and is building up her confidence.

The toy box for special and intense interests

A common discussion with educators is that children with SEND don't necessarily have a wide repertoire of interests in toys and usually tend to have specific and ongoing fascinations. While this might be true to a degree, it is also important to be tuning-in to fleeting moments of curiosity, and mapping what areas and resources a child is most drawn to. The toy box is a good idea for building up a collection of resources based on special and intense interests.

For example, if you have a child that is fascinated by cars or trains, you can set up a toy box based on this and include "extended items" of interest such as train tracks, wheels, different coloured trains and so on. Alternatively, you might find that the interest in the item is about a component or aspect of the toy. For example, is the interest in cars more about the wheels, and the rotation of the wheels, and then your toy box might include items relating to rotation. The purpose of the toy box is to further pique curiosity and to ensure that opportunities are being made for play. The issue that can sometimes emerge with SEND play is that the child is just assumed to be displaying SEND behaviours and fewer efforts are made to understand how this might link to learning.

Reducing distractions

A few years ago, the world sparked joy for Marie Kondo's tidying up methods. Many of the anecdotal reports were that a clear space supports a clear mind, and this concept can be useful for children too. When engaged in thinking and learning, the environment can become hugely distracting. By ensuring that spaces and situations remain clutter-free where possible, children can focus. Of course, there is always space for mess and creativity in the early years, but if, for example, we want the reading corner to be a calm space, we do need to think about how distracting the design, layout and visual noise might be. Less is often more in an early year's space, and so rotating toys, or limiting some resources can actually be beneficial.

Plastic fantastic

Play is diverse and multi-modal, but over recent years, there has been a shift away from commercial or plastic toys because they are considered closeened, and lacking in creative opportunity. Such toys are often invaluable in therapy rooms, because they offer structure and function to children with SEND, and provide cause and effect which can be beneficial for a child building their curiosity and confidence in play. Your environment should strike balance, and many commercial toys feed into children's interests. Cardboard boxes are great but so is Paw Patrol.

Intensive interaction

According to the SENSE charity "Intensive interaction is an approach to helping children and adults who are in the early stages of developing communication and social skills." The premise that the key person mirrors and imitates the child's attempts and expressions of communication through gesture, facial expressions, vocalisations and movements. By acknowledging a child's preferred communication style, and matching it, we are engaging in back and forth interactions that help us to connect with the child, and for them to feel heard. This approach allows you to tune into the child's personal communication, and to build shared experiences. Intensive interactions help educators to value different forms of communication beyond speaking, and helps you to develop a deeper understanding of the child. You can watch and read about examples on the SENSE website (www.sense.org.uk).

SPELL (structure, positivity, empathy, low arousal and links)

SPELL is an evidence-based intervention approach that supports educators to provide optimum learning conditions for neurodivergent children.

Structure

Children with thinking and learning differences and difficulties often benefit from a good degree of structure within both their early learning environment, and the activities and experiences we provide. The use of visuals to describe the sequence of events can be really helpful, and implementing regular routines that support understanding can be really beneficial. The key is to ensure that the child can engage and participate, but if there are no structural cues within the environment, this can become very difficult. Structure should be matched with scaffolding for independence, and so during free or discovery play, using choice boards can provide adequate guidance.

Positivity

Our expectations of all children should be high, and we should be identifying areas of competence as well as supporting areas of need. Build on and recognise children's strengths. A child may accomplish tasks differently to how we would expect or may not do things perfectly each time. Provide positive reinforcement and feedback, and mirror and model ways to play and learn as well.

Empathy (and double empathy)

Children want to be understood, and so leading with empathy is a good skill to develop. Empathy helps us to remove some of the preconceived notions and expectations of children, and instead encourages us to sit with the feelings and experiences of another. Being down at a child's level and seeing the world through their eyes, movement and play is one of the greatest ways to deeply understand the child. Empathy requires uninterrupted time to engage in play connections. This is particularly pertinent for non-speaking children who may have a lot to say through their behaviour; hence we should spend time looking for their emotional, social and communicative cues.

Low arousal

To support play and learning, children need to be in a stress-free state. An environment that is calm, well organised and free from visual and audio clutter provides a foundation for the child's explorations. Some individuals with auditory processing difficulties may require additional time to process information. We may need to pay attention to aversive or distracting stimuli for e.g. noise levels, colour schemes, odours, lighting, clutter etc. Care should be taken not to overload or bombard individuals, which can be made possible by giving clear information that is best suited to them.

Low arousal does not mean "no" arousal. Individuals must be exposed to a range of experiences, but this should be done in a sensitive way considering the fact that they could be over-sensitive to certain stimuli.

Links

When supporting children's play and learning, it is important that there is a shared agreement between those involved with the child's development about how support will be implemented. Too often, educators will carry out strategies and support without fully informing parents, or specialists rely on specialist reports to communicate strategies. Settings should find ways to support strong connections and links with others so that the provision is consistent across different settings.

Novel play materials and modelling

Sometimes it is not about giving up on play and learning, but reinvigorating, extending or adding some basics back into the play. According to Trawick-Smith (2019), children with intellectual disabilities may appear to lose interest in play more quickly, and rather than assume that all is lost with that particular experience or activity, it is important that we spend time offering novel play materials. Within the early years, there has been an explosion of interest in the concept of provocation materials, but rarely do we see this discussed in relation to SEND.

Another thing to consider is that modelling is a strategy that helps a child to see alternative ways of doing things, and so it is good for educators to play alongside, mirror the child's play, but to also state to the child when they decide to do something differently, for example, "I can see that you are lining the cars up, I am going to do it differently and balance them on top of one another." The purpose of this is to help the child to think about the multiple ways a toy or resource will be used.

Play mapping

In his 2018 TED talk, Takaharu Tezuka talked of the importance of designing spaces for children in which they are free to explore the world. During the talk, he shared a visual map of children's movements within a specific time frame. And what was so powerful about this is that children can cover a lot of ground while at play. It is quite common when thinking of children with SEND, that they simply just flit from one space to the other without much play happening, but this isn't necessarily accurate.

Example

Kate had noticed that her key child was very movement based in his play, and she struggled to identify a specific interest because he has very fleeting behaviour. She decided that she would map his movements to see if he was drawn to particular spaces. One day, she drew out a rough map of the indoor and outdoor space and mapped him across the space of 15 minutes. Afterwards, she sat down with the SENCO to analyse his movements. They noticed that he would generally come back-and-forth to a particular space. They observed that he would spend short bursts in the construction space, but as more children gathered in that area, he moved off and came back when he saw that the "coast was clear." They decided that maybe he was drawn to the items in that area but became overwhelmed when surrounded by other children and so they made a small construction box and placed it outdoors where the space was much more open and less crowded. Over time, they noticed that he was beginning to explore the different blocks and was staying within this particular space for long periods. Kate observed him banging the blocks, and he appeared to like the acoustics of the wood.

Strategies to avoid

Changing rooms

I often speak with educators who talk about how much they love changing the room around. It is important to think about how this might impact on a child's sense of emotional safety. Turning up to an entirely re-designed room without proper support and preparation can be a difficult transition. This can be particularly challenging for children with SEND who may rely on familiarity and predictability.

Try not to assume how a space should be used by children; partial or flexible setups allow for children to be guided but also to find their own way with play. For example, don't immediately add chairs around a table, and place carpets under tables so that children know they can use areas functionally and creatively.

SEND friendly spaces

Ensure the environment acts as the third teacher:

- The environment should act as the "third teacher" and make logical sense. For example, using small mats to indicate where a child might play with an item or using arrows to show the direction to places around the space.
- Use labelling across the environment, and ensure it is consistent. Do not over-label as this can be equally as confusing.
- Provide non-speaking feedback and encouragement, for example, thumbs up, smiles and nods.
- Use visual reminders and props to prepare children for a transition.
- Use personalised sequence stories, for example, take pictures of the child engaging in tasks and play, and create a story so that they can view their progress.

Adaptations:

- Adaptations of the environment will be made, and equipment and routine use of additional resources, e.g. Visual Timetables, sand timers, sensory resources etc. as appropriate.
- Provide opportunities for small group work.
- Encourage peer support and interaction.
- Integrate assistive technology where needed.
- Displays and visual noise: use of displays to support learning and remove and limit distractions where possible.

Guided learning:

- Do not bombard the child with language, instructions or verbal expectations.
- Use timers to indicate how long a child has to complete a task.
- Use visuals such as choice boards, sequence cards and examples of the "finished product."
- Play with cause-and-effect toys, e.g. press button toys such as "Jack in a box." Ensure that purposeful actions and sounds from a child are met with a consistent response.

Movement:

- Provide movement breaks, fidgets and sensory items for soothing.
- Treasure baskets and use of natural objects.

Conclusion

One of our key responsibilities as educators is to ensure that children can succeed in their learning. To achieve this, we must ensure that we understand each child's unique threads of thinking. We may need to spend longer periods observing them at play or think beyond conventional definitions of learning to meet the child where they are. Only then can we begin to scaffold a child's learning using their interests and strengths as a springboard. We must also acknowledge that children with learning difficulties will require a deconstructed approach, where we reinterpret what learning looks like based on their individual needs. All children are capable and competent if we are flexible in how we teach key thinking skills. Our provision should support children to build their knowledge through repetition, practice and the time and space to keep trying.

 Read, watch and listen

Executive Function by Centre for the Developing Child Harvard
https://developingchild.harvard.edu/science/key-concepts/executive
-function/

Executive Functions by Encyclopaedia on Early Childhood Development
https://www.child-encyclopedia.com/executive-functions/
introduction

What is Executive Function? by Understood.org
https://www.understood.org/en/learning-thinking-differences/child
-learning-disabilities/executive-functioning-issues/what-is-executive-function

7 | Empowerment and collaboration with parents

Starting points

When I had my first child, I instinctively knew early on that his development wasn't taking the usual route. I was anxious and concerned that I had maybe caused an issue, but I resolved to find out what was happening and to put support in place. I was engaging with the health service and beginning to do some initial research about what could be happening, but it was still an incredibly emotional time, and I was feeling quite fragile. The support of my partner and friends was very much helping, and it was good to have space to process. I decided to take my child to a local nursery as I felt he would benefit from interaction with his peers, which was great for him. I was a little bit nervous about the staff as I didn't yet know them well, and handover times were quite busy, but they made it apparent quite quickly that they too were concerned. They mentioned and followed up with it a lot. They often tried to talk to me about my child and wanted to know lots of personal details about our life, and it all felt a bit too much too soon. I would often go home and research things they had said. I found a social media support group and linked up with some other parents whose children had similar differences. Lots of them helped me understand and celebrate my child. It took so much pressure off to feel understood and supported. Together we were sharing strategies for supporting our children's

DOI: 10.4324/9781003138365-7

development, and it was a comforting place to be. My son's nursery setting decided they wanted to initiate some further referrals for support. I asked if I could look at the paperwork, and in the section about the parents, an educator had written, "mum seems to be in denial, and we are working to help her accept that her child has SEND." I was devastated by the assumption that because I wasn't sharing my whole self with the setting, they decided it meant that I was not processing the situation separately and in spaces where I felt more comfortable. I was not in denial because this suggests that I viewed my child's "SEND" as a problem rather than part of his identity, and this is where the issue can arise in parent partnership.

Reflection questions

- What do you think of this situation?
- What do you think went wrong here, and how might it be resolved?
- Have you heard or engaged with the "in denial narrative?"
- How often do you hear judgements made about parents, their knowledge, engagement and expertise? How do you think this impacts the relationship?
- Have you ever challenged judgements made about parents?

Introduction

Parent partnership is about collaboration, not "surveillance"

The reflection above is taken from a real experience, and it was a very powerful moment because it illustrated the ways in which parent partnerships can be full of unknown or misinterpreted factors, and that actually our judgements or relationships with families can be extremely difficult to navigate. Research consistently highlights that a good partnership leads to good experiences and outcomes for children, but the reality of developing that partnership can be hard. The origins of parent partnership in the early years are quite tricky; for example, Margaret Macmillan was one of the first education pioneers to emphasise the importance of parental involvement, but her approach focused on the ways in which the home environment had deficits and positioned the early years space as the area of expertise (Steedman, 1990). According to Cottle and Alexander (2014), this is a model that remains quite influential, and we often still see the practice of parents being "done to, rather than with." This is particularly pertinent when we think of families with neurodivergent and disabled children especially when we judge them to not be engaging or "hard to reach." The idea that parent partnership should be collaborative has been difficult to achieve because of the positions of power, knowledge and expertise between the educator and the parent. Equally, partnership can sometimes become a form of "surveillance" that checks on parents' engagement, judges it, but rarely seeks to understand why engagement may not be developing.

 DID YOU KNOW?

A study by Hughes and McNaughton (2000) found that educators would often dominate parent partnerships with their own knowledge, thus "othering" parental expertise and knowledge. They identified three forms of othering that potentially impacts the effectiveness of the partnership:

- **Parental knowledge is inadequate:** here, parents are seen as ignorant about what and how to teach their children, and parent involvement programmes rectify this.
- **Parental knowledge is supplementary:** here, parents' knowledge of their child allegedly complements staff's professional knowledge, but in reality merely supplements it.
- **Parental knowledge is unimportant:** here, parents knowledge is not valued as having any significant contribution, thus they become absent in decision-making and collaboration.

This research suggests that we must interrogate our hidden assumptions about parents, particularly when we think about SEND and the intersections such as race, gender and cultural practices. It can feel uncomfortable to acknowledge that we may hold inaccurate judgements about parents, but it is only through transparent reflections that we may come to shift our views regarding the role, potential and knowledge of parents. An important point made by Gonzalez-Mena (1994) is that many educators state that they believe in parent partnership or involvement until the point at which a parent's perspectives and ideas diverge from their own view. This can alter the partnership pretty quickly, and there is no greater disruption to parent partnership than having to navigate conversations based on how well a child is developing.

The partnership can be made fragile because the truth is that we can never assume that we have a deeply embedded partnership with a parent based on the interactions we might have during settling, handovers and updates. I believe that this is something both educators and parents often overestimate. The relationship between an educator and parent can take a long time to build, and it must go beyond the simple systems or procedures of a setting but focus on forming a genuine connection. Educators should be willing to explore that while they bring a professional expertise to the partnership, they also have to embrace the unique identity and personal expertise of the family.

We also have to be very mindful that parents are not a homogenous group, so when developing connections, we have to shift our own perceptions to ensure that we meet parents where they are at. Similarly, educators are not an homogenous group, and so like any partnership, when collaborating in SEND support, each person brings a different set of knowledge, skills, feelings and experience. There is an embedded culture within wider education that the "teacher knows best" but research consistently highlights that when we move away from this power dynamic, our connections with parents and families have much more room to grow, and to be authentic.

Oftentimes, we have to adjust our approach dependent on the child and family in question. Within SEND, it is imperative that we acknowledge that parents may find themselves facing a battleground for the right support and diagnosis, and so we have to carefully consider the difficulties that may emerge if we choose to become defensive against them or seek to control their narrative and lived experience. This tension eventually impacts the child.

Empowerment models

Parental self-efficacy

Parents being knowledgeable and confident in supporting their child's development is essential, especially if there are specific and specialist needs (Macvarish, Lee and Low, 2014). However, research has found that the additional demands of raising a child with special educational needs can exacerbate stress (Crane et al., 2015), and this stress is often caused by the "battles" they face in securing early intervention support (Ryan and Quinlan, 2018). For parents to meet the needs of their child, they must be equipped with the tools and knowledge to understand developmental differences and how best to support learning. Too often, however, parents feel isolated, which can impact their self-belief as a parent, also referred to as parental self-efficacy (PSE).

Parental Self-efficacy is defined as "beliefs or judgements about one's ability to be successful in the role of a parent" (Hess, Teti and Hussey-Gardner, 2004) According to Coleman and Karraker (1998), if a parent feels that they are knowledgeable and confident in their role, they will experience increased PSE levels, and this has a range of benefits, including:

- Increased competency in parenting tasks (Sanders et al., 2003).
- A buffer against stress (Raikes and Thompson, 2005).
- Greater resilience when faced with challenges and adversity (Gelbar, Smith and Reichow, 2014).

PSE levels have also been found to positively impact children's wellbeing outcomes; for example, children are better able to emotionally self-regulate when a parent has good levels of PSE (Purdie, Carroll and Roche, 2004).

However, parents with low PSE are at risk of frustration, stress and depression (Sanders and Woolley, 2005).

As educators, we are also impacted by self-efficacy, and this self-belief can vary depending on the children we are supporting. According to Coleman and Karraker (1998), there are four primary methods of support self-efficacy:

1

Vicarious experience

Parents initially learn through observation of others and then reflecting on their own experiences. When a child has SEND, the parent will need opportunities to observe and understand the child's unique needs, and to have opportunities to observe techniques and strategies in action.

2

Verbal persuasion

Providing feedback has been found to be an effective way to support parental self-efficacy. This feedback is best delivered from trusted others who provide constructive and supportive advice. This should include discussions based on the children's strengths, and interests. Too much feedback about concerns can disempower a parent and lead to disengagement.

3

Psychological and emotional arousal

The parent will also experience physiological/emotional arousal in which their current emotional state informs their self-efficacy. Where this is positive, such as success at their child meeting a milestone like crawling, the parent is likely to continue to face new experiences or challenges without unnecessary stress. However, frequent negative affective states can alleviate stress levels and create avoidance issues as the parent becomes fearful of disappointment or failure (Benedetto and Ingrassia, 2018). Because development looks different in neurodivergence and disability, it is important we adjust our definition of milestones and celebrate the child's unique development.

4

Positive adaptation

As the parent comes to understand their child's diverse development, including learning differences, they can reframe their thinking from a traditional view to a more personalised and adaptive view that more aptly describes their child's particular development. From this, the parent becomes more equipped with new knowledge and skills, thus increasing PSE.

Empowerment Framework

Parent/Carer

Integrates into play,
learning and life skills

Child

Play Rich Experiences

Key Person

Integrates into play,
learning and life skills

Play & Learning Gain

Specialist

Teaches and equips
the parent/carer or
key person

Empowerment paradigm

Souto-Manning and Swick (2006) developed a six-element empowerment paradigm for parent and family involvement, including practices that:

1.   Identify family and child strengths

The most effective way to work with families is to believe in them and look for the good. So often, parents are subject to harsh judgements, or are subject to mounting pressure particularly when a child has SEND. Our role as educators is to advocate for child and family, and so our priority should be to get to know them and to identify strengths that can be built upon.

2.   Validate and engage with parents

When we describe families as "hard to reach," we place the onus and blame on the parent rather than using our empathy lens to connect with the family. There are so many reasons why a family might not engage, so we should reserve making judgements and instead identify what is working. Parents are often told what they need to do or what is not going well. Educators should spend time recognising the efforts of parents and thinking outside the box for engagement. The researchers highlight that engagement may look different across the setting, and that is no bad thing. Parents will value different things, so do not apply blanket expectations, and embrace that families are unique and will engage in different ways and at different paces.

3.   Engagement can exist outside of the setting

Settings can often view lack of engagement with the setting as a lack of engagement full stop. When parents come to our setting, despite how welcoming we may feel we are, there are lots of reasons why a parent might feel out of their comfort zone. Be open to changing location or introducing novel ways to interact. For example, one setting had a monthly children and families walk around a local park. Similarly, home visits can be invasive, so you might suggest meeting somewhere that a parent might feel more comfortable. We must understand that no one model, venue, or format works for every teacher and/or family.

4.   The educator learning alongside the family

The research found that families felt more compelled to form partnerships when the educator expressed that they too were learning within the role. Admitting that you do not know or understand something is not a sign of weakness or incompetence but an indicator of growth. This was particularly important when considering the cultural identity of the child and family. When educators valued the funds of knowledge of children and families, relationships could be built much stronger.

5.   Collaborative schemes and multiple family involvement build trust

It is crucial that educators respond to parent ideas, contributions and feedback, and let parents see educators employing their ideas. Feedback gathering needs to be genuine, well embedded and creative. According to Austin (2000), true collaboration needs to include a real sense of value. Educators should not involve parents because they feel they must, rather they should genuinely want to know and understand their contributions because they can see how this influences the experience of the child. The researchers found that the best collaborations happened when conversations were co-constructed and involved a good balance of tuning-in and listening carefully. Educators and families who would problem-solve and work together to find solutions were able to connect more deeply.

6. Linguistic and cultural appreciation, recognition and reflective responsiveness

Families needed to truly see themselves and their identities within the environment, including language and culture. A diverse range of resources and richness of culture provided a good indicator that the setting is expansive in their provision and not prescribing to one world view or cultural "ideal." This is where we need to also consider where our efforts might seem "tokenistic". For example, having pictures of disabled children with the setting but poor accessibility does not reflect and recognise the reality of disability.

Embracing the empowerment model

It is important to address the idea that a parent and professional have different types of expertise in a child's life. The idea that knowledge must match and be the same is not all that useful and different perspectives provide a richer understanding of the child. The following visual outlines that a) a child is first and foremost the expert in their lived experience, and then the educator possesses a professional knowledge, while the parent possesses a personal knowledge of the child. That is not to say that these forms of knowledge do not intertwine and merge in different ways, but multiple expertise consist of multiple perspectives.

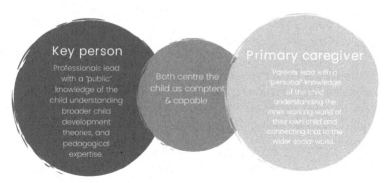

Wellbeing strategies

Wellbeing check-ins

One way of checking how a child might be feeling that day is to have some key wellbeing checkers during handovers. Often, a child's scales might be tipped by any number of things that they cannot necessarily express to us. Knowing this information can help us to establish if a child might feel "out of sorts" that day, and we can then plan and be aware of it. Try asking the parents the following:

* How did the child sleep?

We all know how it feels to have a bad night's sleep, and the same goes for children. Not having adequate rest can impact on our wellbeing.

* Did the child have breakfast?

Breakfast is an important meal and can often set us up for the day, but if the child was reluctant or skipped breakfast, this might impact on mood and wellbeing.

* Did your child go to the toilet this morning?

It may feel like quite an invasive question, but constipation and issues with going to the toilet can impact wellbeing. Imagine the feeling of when you feel bloated and how it can make you feel; the same goes for a child, especially a child who might not be able to explain the feeling or discomfort.

* How was the morning journey into the setting?

Parents often report that transitions can have a big impact on family wellbeing, particularly if things don't go to plan in the morning. For some children, the stress of the morning transition can already feel like a huge emotional toll. Finding out how their morning has been gives you an insight into how the day might go.

Transition spaces

Curtis and Carter (2015) describe a number of ways of creating a sense of belonging and connection in a setting:

Transition kitchen: set up a kitchen or welcome area in the early years space with an adult table, chairs and softenings. The aim is to support parents and children to ease their way into the setting, and to feel that they can linger before they leave. This idea is, of course, dependent on space but is a lovely way to cultivate a culture of welcoming and giving parents time during the handover. It is also a good opportunity for parents to socially network with each other. Similarly, this could be set up in a hallway or nook or cranny.

Communication stations: nursery life can get very busy with lots of comings and goings. Setting up a communication station can be very beneficial for parents who don't always have the time to hang around. They can also become spaces for notes and ideas exchanges. For example, you could have a learning scrapbook, useful guidance, books and leaflets or individual cubbies for letters, work and daily diaries.

Video diaries: the world has become much more technologically savvy since the COVID-19 pandemic, and for parents of children with SEND some of their worries may be around participation, inclusion and belonging. Short video diaries or updates that the parent can watch back are important keepsakes.

READ THE FOLLOWING CASE STUDY:

Toby is an autistic 3-year-old who has been attending a local nursery for six months. The key person has noticed that the morning handover is quite stressful for everyone, and dad always comments that they feel like they have already done a day's work in the morning. This start to the day can impact Toby across the rest of the day as he seems unsettled and overwhelmed by the busy aspects. The key person invites the parents in to discuss ideas, and to think about ways of reducing the morning chaos. Though they are simple ideas, the parents are grateful because they needed some support to think straight. They begin to try the following:

- Wake up ten minutes earlier so they can prepare for the children's wake up time.
- Do not have the television on in the morning, and instead have a few books and a sensory basket out to create a calmer wake up.
- The setting has provided some visuals to help Toby with morning routines such as tooth brushing.
- Toby likes to bring an item along for the walk to nursery but is often told no. This can cause a lot of upset. Instead, they give him a choice of two small items, and it is placed into the home basket once they arrive at the setting.
- The setting benefits from a parent's room and so in the morning they are encouraged when it is available to spend a few minutes gathering themselves before the handover.

This real example highlights the ways in which we can engage in parental advocacy as opposed to judging the parent for the things we might not always see. Parents often rely on educators for their professional knowledge, and so by helping them to problem-solve or come up with solutions can be a real support.

Integrating identity and culture into the setting

EDUCATOR'S VOICE

We have a very diverse setting, and a high number of children with SEND. We continually think about the ways in which we can support children to feel homely when they are in the setting. This includes ways in which we can recognise cultural identities. We were aware that we sometimes relied on tokenistic practices that had little impact or intrinsic value for the child. We implemented the following:

- Sounds bites and videos of parents speaking in their first language, singing nursery rhymes including with Makaton +sign and using slide show photo frames around the setting. This generated so much curiosity.
- We set up a parent music playlist and asked them to add their favourite songs, again, with the idea of language, culture and the joy of dance and movement.
- For transitions into the setting, we complete a family project called "The Museum of Me" and ask parents and the child to choose several items that mean something to them or have a story. This is all placed in an identity box and becomes a conversation starter, which helps us to understand individual identities.
- We reduced our dressing up items and instead had fabric boxes, and we noticed that children began to engage in more critical discussions about identity.

Strategies to avoid

Small boxing

Have a look at your current systems for capturing the parent's "voice," for example, progress checks or planning. You will often find that there are small boxes or areas in which a parent can write their perspectives, but over time this has become quite tokenistic, and is often not filled in. Imagine as a parent how it might feel to see such a small box when it is likely you have so much to say about your child. Consider an ongoing parents "voice" instead, or other creative ways of encouraging parents to initiate and offer their perspectives. Collaborative planning sessions or equally distributed spaces for perspectives is really important for the parent to feel that their voice is welcomed.

Conclusion

Parents and educators are important in supporting the wellbeing of children with SEND. The collaborative efforts between home and the setting can strongly influence the child's experiences, so we must ensure that we adopt an approach that values and celebrates this relationship. This is not to say that it will not be difficult at times, and there may be differences in perspective, but this is not always a bad thing. Recognising that the knowledge a parent and educator has about a child is different only provides us with more opportunities to learn more about that child in various contexts. We must also work hard to ensure that parents feel equal to educators and work with and not against parents. Parents are as much a part of the setting as children and welcoming what they bring will provide a greater opportunity to form a community of support and wellbeing.

 Read, watch and listen

BBC Bitesize Parent's Toolkit – SEND
https://www.bbc.co.uk/bitesize/articles/zh9v382

The School of Life Emotional Education for Children Resources
https://www.theschooloflife.com/home/tools-for-young-minds/

Information Booklet
What to Expect When (Foundation Years)
https://www.foundationyears.org.uk/wp-content/uploads/2019/01/
    What-to-Expect-When-2018.pdf

Parent Toolkit by Ambitious About Autism
https://www.ambitiousaboutautism.org.uk/information-about-autism/
    early-years/parent-toolkit

The Sensory Play Toolkit for Avoidant, Picky or Fussy Eaters
https://sensoryplaytoolkit.weebly.com/

8 | Transition and wellbeing

Starting points

Transition is a ubiquitous and ever-present part of early childhood, and is not just associated with the move to "big school." Research suggests that transitions, whether big or small are stress experiences and can impact on the social and emotional wellbeing of children (Ring and Mhic Mhathúna et al., 2016), in particular children with SEND. We have to carefully consider how we ensure that wellbeing remains at the centre of our practice. Throughout this book, we have considered how the wellbeing scales can be tipped and what we can do to help children with SEND maintain or return to a more balanced stress-free state.

- When you think of transitions, what types of things might tip these scales into disequilibrium?
- Once you have written your list, can you think of the good practices already in place to support children or see gaps within your practice?

As we progress through this chapter, you will consider how you can build upon your skills and knowledge of transition.

Defining transition

There is no universal definition of transition, and it is a contested topic that receives lots of attention and debate. Unfortunately, transition is often singled down to the "big" event of entering school, but it is something that occurs everyday through seemingly mundane routines. It is within these everyday moments, however, that we can create positive transitional experiences that help prepare children for bigger change. Another significant issue is that transition is often discussed with "school readiness" in mind, and so transition becomes confused with academic skills and behavioural conformity suitable for a school environment. However, educators and scholars generally agree that readiness is actually bi-directional and that the school is as much getting ready for the child as they are for the school. This readiness also expands far beyond the traditional expectations of a school and is a preparation for other life events, relationships and experiences. Most importantly, before that "border crossing" of nursery to school even occurs, a child often faces lots of different types of transition, and the child with SEND, without doubt, faces an even greater expanse of transitional experiences.

When beginning to think of a definition or concept for transition, the most important starting point is that the child's identity, experience and "funds of knowledge" must be the starting point for understanding how transitions may shape their social and emotional development. Dunlop (2018) highlighted that transition is not just a single event nor a one-dimensional experience, and children may be situated differently when experiencing that transition. Dunlop illustrates that transitions may:

- Be single or multiple in nature. If transitions are active, and ongoing, it is important to consider how many changes, may be going on for the child.
- Be continuous or discontinuous.
- Suggest readiness or lack of it.
- Highlight resilience or vulnerability.
- Imply agency or lack of control. For example, is an active decision-maker within the transition, or is the transition happening to them. By identifying the difference, we are able to plan for any disruption or emotional discomfort.
- Be visible or silenced.
- Be developmental or socio-cultural.
- Infer that the child be the site of change or conversely that the system should change to accommodate the child.

When we consider this perspective in practice, it is likely that the children with SEND spring to mind because there may be a number of factors that pose a risk to positive change and experience. It is of utmost importance that when supporting children with developmental needs and differences that we consider adapations that will cultivate their safety and wellbeing. Peters and Paki (2014) provide a metaphor of a river to describe transition, which has definition and direction but which also experiences disruptions, curves and different flows. For a child with SEND, these experiences can be more frequent, and the risk of disruption can be greater if we do not plan, prepare and anticipate change.

Types of transitions

Researchers have outlined several types of transitions that occur across early childhood. When we think about children with SEND, there will be additional experiences that will impact the transition, such as attending therapy sessions, or undergoing assessments. Consider the below examples:

Horizontal transitions	Horizontal transitions refer to the daily changes and experiences a child may go through, for example, moving from one activity to another, such as from indoor play to outdoor play. It can include a change in movement or routine.
Micro-transitions	These consist of smaller transitions, such as the educator leaving the room and returning throughout the day. We can sometimes overlook the ebb and flow of these types of transition, but they do come with an emotional impact on the child, particularly if they are not prepared for such uncertainty. According to Kathy Brodie (2018), there can be a real risk that we come to see transitions as practical events and in relation to big milestones such as going to school, but it is within these micro-transitions that children's emotions need to be contained. Micro transitions offer a good opportunity to provide positive experiences which make the bigger changes less daunting.
Vertical transitions	Vertical transitions are much more significant and linked to specific events that do not happen on a regular basis. For example, moving "up" through school.
Associated transitions	This refers to those fewer formal changes in children's lives and routines that occur outside educational settings. These changes may occur in everyday life away from school but can affect and shape children's lives and wellbeing; divorce would be an example of this sort of change as the child may have to move between one parent and another.

(Continued)

(Continued)

| SEND transitions | This refers to the additional experiences a child may need to manage, for example, attending therapy, health appointments, experiencing visitors into the home and setting, medical support, transport support, and wrap around or attendance at specialist and mainstream provision. It is this type of transition that appears to be spoken of less, but indicates additional physical and emotional pressures on the child, and family. |

Adapted from Vogel et al. (2008) and Nutbrown et al. (2013)

 RESEARCH SNIPPETS

- A successful transition can have long-term positive outcomes for children both in their educational success and in terms of social and emotional development, therefore time spent preparing and teaching children to manage transitions is an equitable task (Margetts, 2006; Centre for Excellence and Outcomes in Children and Young People's Services (C4EO), 2010).

- According to Harris, Goodall and Power (2009), there is a wealth of evidence that suggests that parents who support their child's learning and development can have a substantial and positive impact on their children's outcomes. This suggests that settings should develop practices that empower and embrace families personal knowledge, expertise and identity.

- Children with different neurotypes, including Autism, may experience significant difficulty with change and interruptions in routine (Mesibov et al., 2005). They may experience transitions as potential disruptions which conflict with their desire for sameness, familiarity and predictability. This suggests that these aspects should be key features in supporting transition. Ensuring that familiarity exists within change is therefore important. For example, maintaining important routines or rituals for a child.

- Lam and Pollard (2006) conducted observational studies exploring how children react to new spaces. One positive finding was that children show a desire to recreate and reconstruct spaces to meet their own needs and show a sense of active agency during the transition. Educators need to think about "ownership" when planning for transition. Do children enter spaces that clearly do not belong to them, and how much flexibility do we give in allowing this reconstruction?

Transitions are emotions

ACTIVITY

Note down any emotional transitions that you have as an adult experience. How do they make you feel, and how do you manage these transitions?

Examples from other educators:

I drop my children off at school before I head to my nursery for work, and this separation always makes me feel unsettled as I know I will not see them until the evening. We have a little ritual each morning that makes it feel less daunting. My son loves taking something out of my bag and keeping it with him.

I really struggle to leave my home as it is such a cosy place, and so I always take things to work that remind me of home, such as a pair of slippers and my hot chocolate sachets. It sounds silly, but those little moments of comfort during the day make me excited for when I return back to my little nest.

I really miss my partner during the day because she is my safe person. We send texts throughout the day, and I love seeing the messages pop up on my phone on my breaks. Knowing that I have that point of contact is crucial for me to be able to do my job.

Interestingly, these examples mirror what we often will provide for children, and that is comfort and reassurance. The adults plan experiences that remind them of safety, and certainty. If we can make that provision for ourselves and experience emotional transitions as our own lived experiences, this should help us empathise with what it might feel like for a child. One of the key questions to always ask children and families is about the routines and comforts they have at home and establishing that within the setting.

A pedagogy of child empowerment and "voice"

"No decision about me, without me"

There can be a tendency to view transition as an experience that happens to children, and that they don't tend to have much control or say. This can be particularly common when we think of children with SEND but researchers are increasingly finding that transition is better supported when children are actively involved and consulted with about how change may affect their wellbeing. As educators, we need to continue to recognise that prioritising "participation" enhances children's self-esteem

and confidence, promotes their overall development and develops children's sense of autonomy, independence, social competence and resilience (Dewey, 1916; Lansdown, 2005). We also need to challenge the assumption that children with SEND do not have competence, awareness and "voice" because they do not always fit into what we normally expect. It is on us as educators to widen our practices so that children are empowered in the process of transition. The point in planning for a transition is that the disruptions that children experience do not negatively impact their capacity to thrive and develop. Cattaneo and Chapman (2010) propose the process of empowerment that links well to child transitions, and we can use this to consider how we retain children's opportunities for agency, participation, belonging, goal achievement and wellbeing.

The "big" transition – beginnings, endings and beginnings

 DID YOU KNOW?

According to Allen et al. (2018), several studies found that children who develop positive relationships with their early years educators are more positive about attending school, show more excitement for learning and are more self-confident. The implication of this is that conflicted or troubled relationships in the early years setting go on to impact later school experiences, and so time invested in adult–child attachment is never time wasted.

A positive relationship with educators may be especially important for children at risk of academic difficulty because such a relationship can support self-confidence and classroom involvement (Pianta et al., 1995).

There are many types of transition within a child's life, some seeming more significant than others, but all add to a child's understanding of the world and their place within it. Rimm-Kaufman et al. (2000) describe transitions as an exhilarating yet difficult time for both the child and family, and this can be somewhat more difficult when a child has SEND. There are significant shifts in expectations when a child moves through the phases of education, and it is becoming increasingly obvious that the move into compulsory education has bigger demands in a more socially complex environment; for example, parents often express their concerns that children with SEND will be expected to engage with routines that could be overwhelming such as experiencing lunchtime in a large dining space or having break times in large concrete playgrounds. Even more significant is the transition from ratios, and it is here that children with SEND may miss out on that crucial opportunity to feel safe, secure and contained. In short, it is a scary process for many, and adequate planning can make this experience less daunting.

What are children's priorities for setting and "school readiness"?

Children with SEND will experience both the transition into a nursery setting, and to school. One study by Booth (2018) focused on children's perceptions of readiness for school, and through the use of visuals, scales and props, the research found 25 priorities. It is vital that we think beyond just neutotypical development here, but also consider what adaptations and differences we might need to account for in neurodivergence, and disability. Look at the list below, and consider how you might plan for children's priorities.

1. Feeling positive about school and looking forward to going into school.
2. Being enthusiastic and curious about learning.
3. Having a strong sense of self-efficacy and having a strong belief in their own competence.
4. Being able to write, count, read and draw, and the crucial point here is that they can do this not only functionally but creatively.
5. Independence in self-care such as toileting and feeling able to ask for help and to maintain dignity. Be mindful that it can take children longer to develop self-care skills, particularly if they have sensory differences or may not be developmentally ready. Adaptations should be made so that this does not become an additional source of anxiety.
6. Movement including running and balancing, and avoiding accidents.
7. Learning to regulate behaviours and emotions.
8. To cope with transitions, changes and separations.
9. To be able to pay attention and to focus. Be mindful that concepts such as "whole body listening" such as sitting still and giving eye contact are ableist. These skills can look vastly different from child to child.
10. To establish and maintain friends, and resolve conflicts when do they do arise. Be aware here that sometimes you transitional planning will include supporting neurotypical and non-disabled children about different ways of being and learning.
11. Avoid rejections. Be mindful that children with ADHD may experience rejection sensitivity dysphoria (RSD) which makes them extra sensitive to perceived and real rejection.
12. To think and play creatively and to be able to think imaginatively, for pleasure, learning and exploration.

13. To be in a positive pro-social climate, and this should include neurodi-vergent styles of communication.
14. To have predictable routines and guidelines.
15. Supportive and responsive relationships with teachers and caregivers.
16. A strong sense of community.

Empowering parents

Fontil et al. (2019) conducted a systematic review of all the literature relat-ing to transition and special supports for autistic children. Although the focus was on autism, many of the findings suggest that these barriers may be present for different types of developmental differences and indicate a real need for renewed focus on transition for SEND. The review found that educators generally reported not feeling prepared to support and teach chil-dren with special educational needs, and 85% of the articles reported that a collaborative model for transition needs to be adapted. This is often an issue within practice, and educators and teachers alike will often cite that there is no time, capacity or resources to provide meaningful and responsive transi-tions. In addition, the experiences of parents can also be challenging, and if they do not understand the school system, their legal rights and the expecta-tions for inclusive practice, they can be disempowered in knowing how to advocate for educational supports (Fontil and Petrakos, 2015; Hutchinson et al., 2014; Starr et al., 2014). Some suggested solutions could include:

- Viewing transitions as ongoing, and constantly in motion. If we view transitions as just the big events, we can neglect to use the smaller expe-riences as developing a blueprint for the children's resilience and adap-tation to minor and major changes.
- One person does not manage transition; it is often framed as being within an ecological framework with lots of "movement," with each person playing an important role in maintaining consistency.
- Professionals who position parents as a powerful and important force in a child's life promote better psychological health (King et al., 2004), which can positively influence the child.
- Having conversations with the child and family about "what to expect when," and ensuring that you close any information gaps about what children are entitled to across their schooling experience.

- Using evidence-based practice in responsible ways, and balancing this with your knowledge and relationship with the child and family (Westling et al., 2006).

ACTIVITY

During transition "families are often neglected as school staff focus their efforts on children's adaptation in school and less on families' experiences in general" (Fontil and Petrakos, 2015).

- If relationships and partnerships are essential in transition, why do you think they are still so neglected?
- What contingencies does your setting have in place when relationships and partnerships are difficult to establish?

The reason responsive adults are so important in transition is that they introduce the world to the child in "small doses" which gradually builds the child's resilience over time. The issue with too much exposure to or lack of preparedness during transitions means that the child is not able to manage the stress and uncertainty of those experiences. Educators who understand that transition as an intrinsic part of everyday life can build upon their practice to meet a range of needs. We should anticipate that children will have neurodivergent and disabled needs, and begin to think and act upon practice that is inclusive.

Ensuring high expectations for children with SEND

READ THE FOLLOWING CASE STUDY:

When I was working as a reception teacher, I was required to take part in a moderation process so that we could ensure that judgements about children's development were accurate. I would often organise children into key attainment categories such as SEND, EAL and their term of birth. When it came to formal moderation at the end of the year, my local authority moderator chose a child with SEND to moderate, but I told her that there wasn't much point as the child would definitely not reach a good level of development (GLD). The moderator explained that this was even more reason to moderate as it seemed that I had just decided that the presence of SEND meant the child wasn't worth discussing, and that I may have overlooked important aspects of competence. When we explored the child's development, I quickly realised that while he wasn't meeting the goals described, I did have a wealth of examples of his successful development. That day, I realised that the goals at the end of the foundation stage were narrow and ableist, and that it was important for this child's next educator to know his capabilities. The data sets given to the prospective teachers do not always sum up the diverse ways in which our children learn, and so we have to be the advocates of a child during that transition ensuring that information builds knowledge and capacity.

- What is the danger of having low expectations of children with SEND?
- How might we ensure that the next setting or educator is equipped with a knowledge of the child that provides a springboard for their learning?

Celebratory profiles

It is important that when we plan for transition, we use a celebratory framework meaning that we capture a holistic profile of their development. This way, the next key person or teacher has an overall understanding of the child, rather than a plan that focuses purely on their SEND. We should begin with *interests* because we know these offer a springboard for learning, followed by the child's *strengths* and their learning *differences*. We can use this knowledge of the child to plan for their *areas of need* and scaffold their learning and development. This framework encourages us to think more positively about SEND and repositions the child from problem to learner. The celebratory profile below gives you prompts of what you might consider.

Celebratory Framework with Prompts

Key Person 'Voice'

- What do you love about the child?
- What do you hope the child will learn?
- What defines a good day for the child?
- What defines a not so good day?
- What ways do you bond within the setting?

Child's 'Voice'

- What are their preferred forms of communication?
- How do they express their needs?
- How do you know they are engaged?
- What are the signs of disengagement?
- How do they like you to communicate with them?
- What soothes them?
- How do they let you know what they are thinking?

Parent 'Voice'

- What do they love about their child?
- What do they hope their child to learn?
- What defines a good day for the child?
- What defines a not so good day?
- What do they love to do at home with the child?

Strengths & Interests

- What resources and objects do they play with?
- Do they initiate play?
- Which areas do you commonly find them in, for example, areas of continuous provision including whether it is indoors or outdoors
- What are they good at?
- Who do they like to play alongside and with?
- Do they return to particular experiences, or repeat particular types of play?
- What movements do they like to make?
- Who are their favourite people?

Differences

- When thinking of the behaviours which you might usually consider as delayed how do they do it differently to other children? For example, you may have a child that chooses to spin when they want something, rather than to speak.

Areas of Need

- Which area do they need support in:
  Communication & Interaction
  Cognition & Learning
  Social, Emotional and/or Mental Health
  Physical and/or Sensory
- What currently works?
- What is challenging?
- Provide specific examples of what you think they might need

Wellbeing strategies

Adaptations

Children who are D/deaf will experience your setting in a very different way from other children. For example, if you have a "tidy-up" song to get the attention of the children, so they are aware that there is about to be a transition time, how would a child who was hard of hearing be alerted? (Brodie, 2018)

Play passports and transition "headlines"

Information sharing is crucial when a child transitions from one setting to another. It can sometimes feel that the paperwork involved in transition is a tick-box exercise, but what we share with others can be the difference between a smooth or chaotic transition. The play passport, which has been referred to throughout this book, is an idea tool for sharing key information. We are building a picture of the child over time, and there are different aspects of their development that we need to be attuned to, not just their special educational needs or delays, but how they play, communicate, connect, create and share their perspectives.

The play passport serves a number of purposes, including:

- Developing a celebratory profile of the child's strengths, interests, differences and needs.
- It is a capacity building tool for the next educator or important person in that child's life.
- It is an inclusive document that recognises all forms of identity and learning, not just those outlined in developmental statements or goals.
- It increases opportunities for the child to be heard, understood and enabled to thrive and succeed with support and independently.

It is not ... another piece of paperwork to fill in.

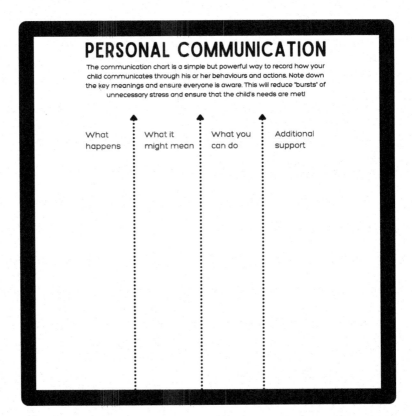

PERSONAL COMMUNICATION

The communication chart is a simple but powerful way to record how your child communicates through his or her behaviours and actions. Note down the key meanings and ensure everyone is aware. This will reduce 'bursts' of unnecessary stress and ensure that the child's needs are met!

What happens	What it might mean	What you can do	Additional support

Another useful tool is the transition "headlines." When speaking with an educator, they shared that sometimes they simply do not have the time right away to read every single piece of information, so knowing the key "headlines" can be crucial. The example attached highlights the type of information you might include:

TRANSITION HEADLINES

Example

1. Charlie engages in stimming behaviours when he is excited, and will usually flap his arms. He should not be stopped from doing this as it helps him to regulate his emotions

2. Charlie is non-verbal but is very responsive to intensive interaction. When you mirror his movements, he will respond positively and often seek forr this to be repeated.

3. Charlie loves peas, toast and bananas. He will usually join in with group meal times if one of these good items is available. Try not to mix foods together on his plate. He likes them to be separate.

4. Charlie absolutely adores sea creatures and has a large collection at home. Incorporating any resources that feature the sea, boats and creatures will get him engaged.

5. If Charlie is sad, he likes to have his comfort item nearby. He has a teddy called Jaws and if you offer this to him, he likes to access this independently from his bag.

6. If Charlie needs help, he will often take hold of your hand, or gain attention by holding your face. This is his way of letting you know that he needs support. Acknowledging this communication helps him to regulate and wait.

Social stories

Carol Gray (1991, 2015) coined the term "social stories," which are concrete and literal descriptions of settings, events and activities in a story format. They are used to assist a child with SEND in understanding and developing their understanding. It is important, however, that social stories are not used to teach neurotypical skills, and should be used to guide and embrace the child's unique way of learning. They can explain why and how things happen, which helps the child prepare for transitions and new experiences. They also can help with sequencing (what comes next in a series of activities) and "executive functioning" (planning and organising).

They can be used in a number of ways, including:

- Teaching self-care skills such as learning to brush teeth or wash hands.
- The development of social skills, for example, asking for help, play entry or indicating a need.
- To demonstrate the expected sequence of a situation.
- To provide a unique perspective of the neurodivergent perspective, for example, a story about sensory processing or how to find calm.
- To prepare for transitions and changes, for example, travelling from home to nursery.
- To celebrate, acknowledge and provide feedback about strengths, achievements and milestones.
- A behavioural support, such as what to do when upset.

Social stories provide predictability and structure for a child and thereby reduce anxiety by offering knowledge about what might happen in a specific situation as well as helping the child to know what to expect. They are ideal for transitional support, and the personal element means that you can plan for the child's individual needs. Social stories can also be used between peers so that children learn about differences, and how to navigate neurodivergence.

Family stories

CASE STUDY

In our setting, we developed something called "Family Stories." While it is important to diversify your bookshelf, sometimes it can be really beneficial to personalise books so that the children learn about themselves and each other. We really engaged the children and parents and set up a family story workshop. The books were laminated for safekeeping and included a rich tapestry of each child's identity, including their family story. These books transitioned with the children and were utilised for information sharing. We learnt more about the child and family in one that workshop than we ever could with an "All About Me" form.

Story drawing

A great way to spend some quality time together is to ask your children to tell you a story and draw it out as they tell it. Bringing children's thoughts and imagination to life can help them to process information. You can even switch roles and encourage your child's storytelling.

Child's "voice"

When we consider "bigger" transitions, if we want to ensure that children's perspectives and voices are heard, it is important we develop creative ways of gathering thoughts and opinions, including from non-speaking children. Researchers have begun to consider how the voices of children can inform our understanding of their experiences, and this can also be used in our everyday practice. For example, developing scales, or resources that help us to gain an insight into the child's thoughts and feelings can be really beneficial. For example, if the child goes up for a visit to "big school," try a likes and dislikes scale activity afterwards so that the child can indicate what works and what does not.

How happy are you?

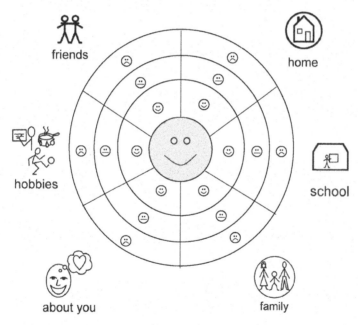

Thinking about everything we've talked about, on a scale of 0 to 10, where 10 is being as happy as you could be... where are you now?

The "just one" strategy

It can feel overwhelming when we are trying to ensure that a child settles into a new space and develops a sense of belonging. One of the key issues that can emerge is that educators set themselves too many tasks to make this happen. The "just one" strategy encourages a more mindful approach to transition, recognising that it takes time to settle, and that by focusing on key transition experiences, the child has the time and space to adapt. Below are just a few examples of the areas of focus you might "just one" on.

- Ensuring objects of transition and transitional objects support the child, and meet their emotional, and sensory needs.
- Developing a connection with a familiar adult through uninterrupted quality time.
- Playing alongside and with another child.
- Engaging in an activity or experience of interest.
- Developing curiosity or beginning to explore the environment.
- Developing the safety and security to relax.
- Developing independence in an activity or task.
- Indicating needs and wants.

SEND friendly spaces

- **Routines and rhythms:** ask the parents about objects, routines and rhythms that create a sense of familiarity. Mirroring experiences can be powerful in supporting the child to feel safe. Where possible, offer additional visits and settling-in sessions so that the child can become accustomed to the routines and rhythms within the setting.
- **Occupational skills:** check with the family or previous setting whether there are any occupational skills that the child needs support with, for example, a photo routine for handwashing, or particular ways of carrying out routines.
- **Sensory safety:** many children with developmental differences also have sensory needs. It is important to establish what the child is over-responsive and under-responsive to. For example, are they triggered by certain sounds or smells, or do they seek out certain sensory experiences. By planning for this, you can plan for and create sensory safety.
- **Comfort objects:** ensure the child has access to comfort items and transitional objects. Speak to the family about objects of safety and make a transition basket.

(Continued)

(Continued)

- **The environment:** the environment should cultivate independence, and so ask yourself whether the lay out and routines make sense? For example, sequenced routines on the wall or labels with visuals and symbols.
- **Celebratory profile:** use a celebratory profile to share a holistic profile of the child that celebrates interests, strengths, differences and supports areas of need.
  Getting to know you:
  - Create an educator one-page profile to introduce yourself.
  - During the settling-in period, provide the family with a setting object of transition so that the family can utilise this at home to talk about the setting. Something simple such as a painted pebble can help, and travel to and from the setting with the child.
  - Record a video message for the child and family, which could include a show round of the environment. This is something the child and parent can watch back together.
  - Use parents' names to build trust.
  - Introduce social and personal stories early on, and where possible include key information about transitions. For example, request images from the school and use these to create a story sequence.
  - Introducing the school uniform early so that the child can become accustomed to the materials, occupational skills of getting dressed and consider, if there will be any sensory diet adaptations needed.
  - Use a personal communication dictionary for any child that is non-speaking or minimally verbal. Fill this in together with the family so that the child's individual communication style is understood.

Conclusion

Transition and change are inevitable, not only in the early years but across our lifespan. Going through the motions of an emotional or physical transition can be disruptive and stressful, but in the context of the "right relationships," they can also be positive and transformative experiences. In the early years phase, we have ample opportunity to support children to positively experience change and develop resilience. We must also acknowledge that transitions happen to the adults in a child's life and that there is a lot of emotional management throughout these processes. We have a responsibility throughout transitions to ensure that everyone is equipped with the tools and information to succeed. Transition should be viewed as a continual and ongoing process in which we are always finding ways to navigate our way through. This way, the bigger milestones won't seem so daunting.

Read, watch and listen

Early Years SEND Partnership Resources by Council for Disabled Children
https://councilfordisabledchildren.org.uk/early-years-send-partner-ship/training-resources-and-support/early-years-send-partnership-resources

Child's "Voice" Toolkit
http://www.socialworkerstoolbox.com/category/wishes-feelings-2/

Guidance for Social Stories
https://www.autism.org.uk/advice-and-guidance/topics/commu-nication/communication-tools/social-stories-and-comic-strip-coversations

Social Story Sampler
https://carolgraysocialstories.com/social-stories/social-story-sampler/

The Ultimate Guide to Transitions Blog
https://inclusiveteach.com/2017/07/29/the-ultimate-guide-to-transitions/

Concluding remarks and a word on advocacy

Advocacy and agency

Over the past few years, I have been lecturing on an early education degree. I usually find that my teaching is focused on how students can develop a strong enough professional identity to face the oppositional forces that challenge and create barriers within our sector. Educators spend much of their time navigating systems that don't necessarily always work in the best interests of children and families, and it is often the case that they need to be doing more and more with less and less. Whether that be funding cuts, shortage of time, capacity or whole team skill sets, it can be easy to feel overwhelmed by some of the challenging aspects of our sector. This sense of being overwhelmed can be compounded even further when we feel the weight of responsibility to ensure that all our children and families get what they need to thrive.

Despite these challenges, educators still turn up every day and fulfil the role to the best of their ability. While the differences that we make may not always feel enough, we know that things can shift in the right direction with each intentional and informed action we take. Educators often overlook how significant their caregiving and teaching has in shaping children's sense of self, identity and wellbeing. It can sometimes feel as though the early years is the "school readiness" waiting room, and that what we do isn't hugely important or influential. The quality of our love, care and support, however, can become the internal working model for the child, and so we have to get it right. Our belief in children's competence and capabilities can be a powerful force in supporting their lifelong learning characteristics. If the early years' experience for a child with

SEND is one of adversity and low expectations, they might always feel like they are trailing behind others rather than forging their own path. As educators, our core principle is to celebrate the unique child, and so we must use our sense of agency to ensure that we advocate for the rights of every child, which will eventually help them to engage in their own self-advocacy. We can choose to reject the things that do not uphold these rights. For example, speaking up when we hear children with SEND described in deficit only terms. All these small acts make a difference to the wellbeing of our children and ourselves. Research has found that advocacy is good for us because:

- It improves the quality of life for others (Mitchell and Philibert, 2002; Seitler, 2007).
- It enriches the lives of children, challenges injustices and promotes overall welfare and wellbeing (Pithouse and Crowley, 2007).
- It can stop feelings of disempowerment and ensure we do not become stagnant within our roles. Advocacy helps us to retain a sense of competence and purpose (Jalongo, 2002).

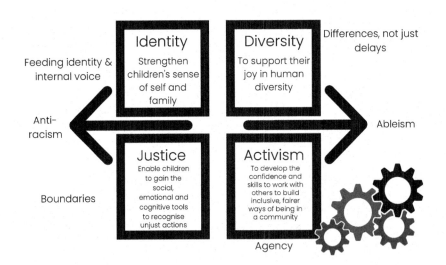

What next for wellbeing?

When writing this book, I found myself digging deep for information relating to wellbeing, neurodiversity and SEND in the early years. Many of the topics and ideas shared throughout this book have been accumulated through real-life everyday practice. For many, the development of skills and expertise in SEND happen "on the job." The work is deeply emotional and relational, and we need a strong underpinning foundation of what will work best for children's wellbeing and development. That is not to say we should be dominated by evidence-based practice; rather, we use it to guide, shape and mould around the very real lived experiences of the child. We need to be adequately prepared for the diverse ways children learn, to connect with their worlds, and we need to have a clear grasp of how we can help or hinder that development. Many of the strategies and ideas can only be effective if they are delivered in the context of warm, responsive and tuned-in relationships. For me, that is the key to wellbeing in SEND. The child and family need to know we are on their side, even when it can be challenging. The most valuable currency we can offer is the presence of ourselves, our empathy and our understanding. We will at times feel vulnerable because so much of the SEND support we offer is accompanied by the unknown or having to navigate things we do not feel entirely confident in, but there is power and connection in that vulnerability. And so, the next thing for wellbeing is to take from this book the strategies and techniques that can add to your current toolkits. Build upon your practice and look after yourself to be able to look after the children in your care. I am going to end on a quote that inspires me daily as a reminder that our influence is powerful:

> I've come to a frightening conclusion that I am the decisive element in the classroom. It's my personal approach that creates the climate. It's my daily mood that makes the weather. As a teacher, I possess a tremendous power to make a child's life miserable or joyous. I can be a tool of torture or an instrument of inspiration. I can humiliate or heal. In all situations, it is my response that decides whether a crisis will be escalated or de-escalated, and a child humanized or dehumanized.
>
> (Ginnott, 1993, np)

Final reflection

Throughout this book, you will have hopefully identified lots of familiar ideas that are already present within your practice and considered the ways in which you can build up on your knowledge and expertise of SEND and wellbeing. For the final reflection, note down the following:

1. List three things that you were already doing and that you consider a key strength.
2. List two things that you will stop doing or will adapt.
3. List three things you will start doing to continue building on your practice.

Within SEND, it is crucial to remember that you are likely already engaged in lots of practice supportive of wellbeing. It is important to be aware of what you already do well and consider how you can build upon this to further strengthen your practice. Educators do not celebrate or recognise their strengths enough because they can often feel that there is always more to learn and do. In the same way that we refer to children's learning journey's, we too continue to professionally develop across our work with children and families. While much can be unknown as we initially begin working with children and families, our curiosity to learn about their identity, culture and funds of knowledge opens a gateway for inclusive practice. Return to the above list regularly, and what you will likely identify is that your practice is ever-changing and expanding. The willingness to adapt and be responsive to children's unique needs ultimately builds better futures for ourselves and our children.

Answers

Read the following scientific statements about neuroscience. Which do you believe to be true, and which do you believe to be false?

- We only use 10% of our brain. **(false)**
- Individuals learn better when they receive information in their preferred learning style (e.g. auditory, visual, kinaesthetic). **(false)**
- Differences in hemispheric dominance (left brain, right brain) can help explain individual differences among learners. **(false)**
- Children are less attentive after consuming sugary drinks and/or snacks. **(false)**
- Learning problems associated with developmental differences in brain function cannot be remediated by education. **(false)**
- A common sign of dyslexia is seeing letters backwards. **(false)**
- Listening to classical music increases children's reasoning ability. **(false)**
- Everything that is important for brain development occurs within the first three years. **(false)**
- Following a specific diet can help overcome certain neurological disabilities, such as ADHD, dyslexia and autism spectrum disorders. **(false)**
- Doing basic Brain Gym exercises help students to learn to read and use language better. **(false)**

(Torrijos-Muelas et al., 2021)

References

Allen, G. (2011). *Early intervention: The next steps, an independent report to Her Majesty's government by Graham Allen MP*. The Stationery Office, London.

Almond L., and Lambden K. (2016). *Promoting purposeful physical play in the early years through physical literacy. A self-learning programme for early years settings and their educators*. Step into Purposeful Play.

Austin J. E. (2000). *The collaboration challenge*. Jossey Bass.

Austin, R. D., and Pisano, G. P. (2017). Neurodiversity as a competitive advantage. *Harvard Business Review, 95*(3), 96–103.

Aylward, P., and O'Neill, M. (2009). *Invest to grow. Final evaluation report, through the looking glass – A community partnership in parenting*. Commonwealth Department of Family and Community Services and Indigenous Affairs. Retrieved 28 October 2010, from https://www.adelaide.edu.au/directory/paul.aylward?dsn=directory.file;field=data;id=6772;m=view.

Bayat, M. (2019). *Addressing challenging behaviors and mental health issues in early childhood*. Routledge.

Bayer, J. K., Hiscock, H., Ukoumunne, O. C., Price, A., and Wake, M. (2008). Early childhood aetiology of mental health problems: A longitudinal population-based study. *Journal of Child Psychology and Psychiatry, 49*(11), 1166–1174.

Benedetto, L., and Ingrassia, M. (Eds.). (2018). *Parenting: Empirical advances and intervention resources*. BoD–Books on Demand.

Bercow, J. (2018). Bercow: Ten years on: An independent review of provision for children and young people with speech, language and communication needs in England. www.bercow10yearson.com/wp-content/uploads/2018/03/337644-ICAN-Bercow-Report-WEB.pdf

Berk, L. E., and Meyers, A. B. (2013). The role of make-believe play in the development of executive function: Status of research and future directions. *American Journal of Play, 6*(1), 98–110.

Bhat, A. N., and Srinivasan, S. (2013). A review of "music and movement" therapies for children with autism: Embodied interventions for multisystem development. *Frontiers in Integrative Neuroscience, 7*, 22.

Biel, L., and Paske, N. K. (2005). *Raising a sensory smart child. The definitive handbook for helping your child with sensory integration issues.* Penguin Group.

Biel, L., and Peske, N. (2009). *Raising a sensory smart child: The definitive handbook for helping your child with sensory processing issues.* Penguin.

Biringen, Z., Altenhofen, S., Aberle, J., Baker, M., Brosal, A., Bennett, S.,... and Swaim, R. (2012). Emotional availability, attachment, and intervention in center-based child care for infants and toddlers. *Development and Psychopathology, 24*(1), 23–34.

Booth, A. (2018). Children's own priorities for their school readiness. *Children's Research Network.* https://www.childrensresearchnetwork.org/knowledge/resources/childrens-own-priorities-for-their-school-readiness

Bowlby, J., (1988). *A secure base: Parent-child attachment and healthy human development.* Basic Books.

Brackett, M. A., Palomera, R., Mojsa-Kaja, J., Reyes, M. R., and Salovey, P. (2010). Emotion-regulation ability, burnout, and job satisfaction among British secondary-school teachers. *Psychology in the Schools, 47*(4), 406–417.

Bridgeland, J., Bruce, M., and Hariharan, A. (2013). *The missing piece: A national survey on how social and emotional learning can empower children and transform schools.* Washington, DC: Civic Enterprises. Retrieved from http://www.civicenterprises.net/MediaLibrary/Docs/CASEL-Report-low-res-FINAL.pdf.

Brodie, K. (2018). *The holistic care and development of children from birth to three: An essential guide for students and educators.* Routledge.

Brodin, J., and Renblad, K. (2020). Improvement of preschool children's speech and language skills. *Early Child Development and Care, 190*(14), 2205–2213.

Brooks, R. (2019). *The trauma and attachment-aware classroom: A practical guide to supporting children who have encountered trauma and adverse childhood experiences.* Jessica Kingsley Publishers.

Brunsting, N. C., Sreckovic, M. A., and Lane, K. L. (2014). Special education teacher burnout: A synthesis of research from 1979 to 2013. *Education and Treatment of Children,* 681–711.

Buettner, C. K., Jeon, L., Hur, E., and Garcia, R. E. (2016). Teachers' social–emotional capacity: Factors associated with teachers' responsiveness and professional commitment. *Early Education and Development, 27*(7), 1018–1039.

Butchart, A., Harvey, A. P., Mian, M., Fürniss, T., and Kahane, T. (2006). *Preventing child maltreatment: A guide to taking action and generating evidence.* France: World Health Organization and International Society for Prevention of Child Abuse, WHO Press, World Health.

Carnevali, L., Montano, N., Statello, R., Coudé, G., Vacondio, F., Rivara, S.,... and Sgoifo, A. (2017). Social stress contagion in rats: Behavioural, autonomic and neuroendocrine correlates. *Psychoneuroendocrinology, 82,* 155–163.

Cattaneo, L. B., and Chapman, A. R. (2010). The process of empowerment: A model for use in research and practice. *American Psychologist, 65*(7), 646–659. https://doi.org/10.1037/a0018854

CECE (2019). Practice guideline: Inclusion of children with disabilities. https://www.college
-ece.ca/en/Documents/Practice_Guideline_Inclusion.pdf

Centre for Excellence and Outcomes in Children and Young People's Services (C4EO).
(2010). *Ensuring that all children and young people make sustained progress and
remain fully engaged through all transitions between key stages.* Retrieved November
2013, from http://archive.c4eo.org.uk/pdfs/3/Schools%20and%20 Communities
%20KR%20P2.pd

Chang, Y. C., Shih, W., Landa, R., Kaiser, A., and Kasari, C. (2018). Symbolic play in school-
aged minimally verbal children with autism spectrum disorder. *Journal of Autism and
Developmental Disorders, 48*(5), 1436–1445.

Child's Play Therapy Center (n.d.). What is 'heavy work' for children and how does it help?
https://www.childsplaytherapycenter.com/what-is-heavy-work-for-children-and-how
-does-it-help/

Charlop, M. H., Lang, R., and Rispoli, M. (2018). *Play and social skills for children with
autism spectrum disorder.* Springer.

Cigala, A., Venturelli, E., and Bassetti, M. (2019). Reflective practice: A method to improve
teachers' well-being. A longitudinal training in early childhood education and care
centers. *Frontiers in Psychology, 10,* 2574.

Clemens, S. L., and Lincoln, D. J. (2018). Where children play most: Physical activity levels
of school children across four settings and policy implications. *Australian and New
Zealand Journal of Public Health, 42*(6), 575–581.

Cohen, L., and Uhry, J. (2007). Young children's discourse strategies during block play:
A Bakhtinian approach. *Journal of Research in Childhood Education, 21*(3), 302–315.

Coleman, P. K., and Karraker, K. H. (1998). Self-efficacy and parenting quality: Findings
and future applications. *Developmental Review, 18*(1), 47–85.

Coleman, P. K., and Karraker, K. H. (2003). Maternal self-efficacy beliefs, competence in
parenting, and toddlers' behavior and developmental status. *Infant Mental Health
Journal: Official Publication of The World Association for Infant Mental Health, 24*(2),
126–148.

Comer, James (1995). https://theeffortfuleducator.com/2018/05/09/relationships-and
-learning-clarification-on-a-popular-quote/.

Community Playthings (n.d.). A good place to be two. https://www.communityplaythings
.co.uk/learning-library/training-resources/a-good-place-to-be-two

Connell, G., and McCarthy, C. (2013). *A moving child is a learning child: How the body
teaches the brain to think (birth to age 7).* Free Spirit Publishing.

Connell, G., and McCarthy, C. (2014). *A moving child is a learning child: How the body
teaches the brain to think (birth to age 7).* Free Spirit Publishing.

*Conversations on love: With Philippa Perry, Dolly Alderton, Roxane Gay, Stephen Grosz,
Esther Perel, and many more.* Viking.

Cottle, M., and Alexander, E. (2014). Parent partnership and "quality" early years services:
Educators' perspectives. *European Early Childhood Education Research Journal, 22*(5),
637–659.

Crane, L., Batty, R., Adeyinka, H., Goddard, L., Henry, L. A., and Hill, E. L. (2018). Autism diagnosis in the United Kingdom: Perspectives of autistic adults, parents and professionals. *Journal of Autism and Developmental Disorders, 48*(11), 3761–3772.

Crane, L., Chester, J. W., Goddard, L., Henry, L. A., and Hill, E. (2015). Experiences of autism diagnosis: A survey of over 1000 parents in the United Kingdom. *Autism, 20*(2), 153–162.

Curtis, D., and Carter, M. (2014). *Designs for living and learning: Transforming early childhood environments*. Minnesota: Redleaf Press.

Department for Education (DfE) (2014). "Early years: Guide to the 0 to 25 SEND code of practice," https://assets.publishing.service.gov.uk/government/uploads/system/uploads/attachment_data/file/350685/Early_Years_Guide_to_SEND_Code_of_Practice_-_02Sept14.pdf

Department for Education and Department of Health. (2015) *Special educational needs and disability code of practice: 0 to 25 years*. Available at: https://assets.publishing.service.gov.uk/government/uploads/system/uploads/attachment_data/file/398815/SEND_Code_of_Practice_January_2015.pdf.

Department for Education (DfE) (2016). https://assets.publishing.service.gov.uk/government/uploads/system/uploads/attachment_data/file/575632/Mental_health_of_children_in_England.pdf.

Department for Education (DfE) (2020). "Early years foundation stage reforms," https://assets.publishing.service.gov.uk/government/uploads/system/uploads/attachment_data/file/896872/EYFS_reforms_consultation_-_government_response.pdf

Department for Education (DfE) (2021). "Changes to the early years foundation stage (EYFS) framework," www.gov.uk/government/publications/changes-to-the-early-years-foundation-stage-eyfs-framework/changes-to-the-early-years-foundation-stage-eyfs-framework

Department for Education (DfE) and Department of Health (DoH) (2015). "Special educational needs and disability code of practice: 0 to 25 years," https://assets.publishing.service.gov.uk/government/uploads/system/uploads/attachment_data/file/398815/SEND_Code_of_Practice_January_2015.pdf

Department for Work and Pensions and Cabinet Office (2011). Early intervention: The next steps. https://www.gov.uk/government/publications/early-intervention-the-next-steps--2.

Derman-Sparks, L., Edwards, J. Olsen, and Goins, C. M. (2020). *Anti-bias education for young children and ourselves* (2nd ed.). National Association for the Education of Young Children.

Derman-Sparks, L., and Edwards, J. O. (2021). Teaching about identity, racism, and fairness: Engaging young children in anti-bias education. *American Educator, 44*(4), 35–40.

Devarakonda, C. (2012). *Diversity and inclusion in early childhood: An introduction*. Sage.

Dewey, J. (1916). *Democracy and education: An introduction to the philosophy of education*. MacMillan.

DfE. (2015). *SEND code of practice 0–25 years*. Department for Education, Department of Health, 216–229.

Dodge, R., Daly, A. P., Huyton, J., and Sanders, L. D. (2012). The challenge of defining wellbeing. *International Journal of Wellbeing*, 2(3), 222–235. https://doi.org/10.10.5502 /ijw.v2i3.4

Dunlop, A. W. (2018). *Transitions in early childhood education*. Oxford University Press.

Dunst, C. (2012). Effects of puppetry on elementary students' knowledge of and attitudes toward individuals with disabilities. *International Electronic Journal of Elementary Education, 4*, 451–457.

Early Education (2012). Development matters in the Early Years Foundation Stage (EYFS). www.foundationyears.org.uk/files/2012/03/Development-Matters-FINAL-PRINT -AMENDED.pdf

Early Years Alliance (2018) Minds matter: The impact of working in the early years sector on practitioners' mental health and wellbeing. Available at: www.eyalliance.org.uk/ sites/default/files/minds-matter-report-.pdf (accessed 22 March 2021).

Ebbeck, M., Phoon, D. M. Y., Tan-Chong, E. C. K., Tan, M. A. B., and Goh, M. L. M. (2015). A research study on secure attachment using the primary caregiving approach. *Early Childhood Education Journal, 43*(3), 233. https://doi.org/10.1007/s10643-014-0647-4

Elfer, P. (2012). Emotion in nursery work: Work discussion as a model of critical professional reflection. *Early Years, 32*(2), 129–141.

Elyatt, W. (2020). *The ecology of wellbeing*. The Flourish Project.

Erdman, S. Colker, L. J., and Winter, E. C. (2020). Preventing compassion fatigue: Caring for yourself. *NAEYC*. https://www.naeyc.org/resources/pubs/yc/jul2020/preventing -compassion-fatigue

Ereaut, G., and Whiting, R. (2008). *What do we mean by "wellbeing"?: And why might it matter?* Department for Children, School and Families.

Felitti, V. J., Anda, R. F., Nordenberg, D., Williamson, D. F., Spitz, A. M., Edwards, V., and Marks, J. S. (1998). Relationship of childhood abuse and household dysfunction to many of the leading causes of death in adults: The Adverse Childhood Experiences (ACE) Study. *American Journal of Preventive Medicine, 14*(4), 245–258.

Fisher, J. (2016). *EBOOK: Interacting or interfering? Improving interactions in the early years*. McGraw-Hill Education (UK).

Fontil, L., and Petrakos, H. H. (2015). Transition to school: The experiences of Canadian and immigrant families of children with autism spectrum disorders. *Psychology in the Schools, 52*(8), 773–788. https://doi.org/10.1002/pits.21859.

Fontil, L., Gittens, J., Beaudoin, E., and Sladeczek, I. E. (2020). Barriers to and facilitators of successful early school transitions for children with autism spectrum disorders and other developmental disabilities: A systematic review. *Journal of Autism and Developmental Disorders, 50*(6).

Frederickson, N., and Dunsmuir, S. (2009). *Measures of children's mental health and psychological wellbeing: A portfolio for education and health professionals*. Granada Learning.

Freeman, S. F., and Kasari, C. (2002). Characteristics and qualities of the play dates of children with down syndrome: Emerging or true friendships? *American Journal on Mental Retardation, 107*(1), 16–31.

Friedman, C., and Owen, A. L. (2017). Defining disability: Understandings of and attitudes towards ableism and disability. *Disability Studies Quarterly, 37*(1).

Friedman, N. P., and Miyake, A. (2004). The relations among inhibition and interference control functions: A latent-variable analysis. *Journal of Experimental Psychology: General, 133*(1), 101.

Friedman, N. P., and Miyake, A. (2017). Unity and diversity of executive functions: Individual differences as a window on cognitive structure. *Cortex, 86*, 186–204.

Frivold Kostøl, E. M., and Cameron, D. L. (2020). Teachers' responses to children in emotional distress: A study of co-regulation in the first year of primary school in Norway. *Education, 3–13*, 1–11.

Fuster, J. M. (2013). Cognitive functions of the prefrontal cortex. *Principles of Frontal Lobe Function*, 11–22.

Fuster, J. (2015). *The prefrontal cortex*. Cambridge, MA: Academic Press.

Garnett, H. (2017). *Developing empathy in the early years: A guide for educators*. Jessica Kingsley Publishers.

Gasper, D. (2010). Understanding the diversity of conceptions of well-being and quality of life. *The Journal of Socio-Economics, 39*(3), 351–360.

Gasper, M., and Walker, R. (Eds.). (2020). *Mentoring and Coaching in Early Childhood Education*. Bloomsbury Publishing.

Gelbar, N. W., Smith, I., and Reichow, B. (2014). Systematic review of articles describing experience and supports of individuals with autism enrolled in college and university programs. *Journal of Autism and Developmental Disorders, 44*(10), 2593–2601.

Gernsbacher, M. A., and Yergeau, M. (2019). Empirical failures of the claim that autistic people lack a theory of mind. *Archives of Scientific Psychology, 7*(1), 102.

Gillespie, L. (2015). The role of co-regulation in building self-regulation skills. *Young Children*, 94.

Goerlich, K. S. (2018). The multifaceted nature of alexithymia–a neuroscientific perspective. *Frontiers in psychology, 9*, 1614.

Gonzalez-Mena J. (1994). *From a parent's perspective*. Salem, WI: Sheffield.

Goleman, D., and Davidson, R. (2017). *The science of meditation: How to change your brain, mind and body*. Penguin UK.

Graham, B., White, C., Edwards, A., Potter, S., and Street, C. (2019). *School exclusion: A literature review on the continued disproportionate exclusion of certain children*. Department for Education.

Gray, C. (2015) *The new social story book: 15th anniversary edition*. Future Horizons Firm.

Gross, J. J. (1998). The emerging field of emotion regulation: An integrative review. *Review of General Psychology, 2*(3), 271–299.

Guo, Y., Leu, S.-Y., Barnard, K. E., Thompson, E. A., and Spieker, S. J. (2015). An examination of changes in emotion co-regulation among mother and child dyads during the strange situation. *Infant and Child Development, 24*(3): 256–273. https://doi.org/10.1002/icd.1917.

Hamre, B. K., and Pianta, R. C. (2005). Can instructional and emotional support in the first-grade classroom make a difference for children at risk of school failure? *Child Development, 76*(5), 949–967.

Hanscom, A. J. (2016). *Balanced and barefoot: How unrestricted outdoor play makes for strong, confident, and capable children.* New Harbinger Publications.

Harris, A., and Goodall, J. (2009). Helping families support children's success at school (London, save the children).

Heiskanen, N., Alasuutari, M., and Vehkakoski, T. (2018). Positioning children with special educational needs in early childhood education and care documents. *British Journal of Sociology of Education, 39*(6), 827–843.

Heschong, L., Wright, R. L., and Okura, S. (2002). Daylighting impacts on human performance in school. *Journal of the Illuminating Engineering Society, 31*(2), 101–114.

Hess, C. R., Teti, D. M., and Hussey-Gardner, B. (2004). Self-efficacy and parenting of high-risk infants: The moderating role of parent knowledge of infant development. *Journal of Applied Developmental Psychology, 25*(4), 423–437.

Honig, A. S. (2007). Oral language development. *Early Child Development and Care, 177*(6–7), 581–613.

Howes, C. (2000). Social-emotional classroom climate in child care, child-teacher relationships and children's second-grade peer relations. *Social Development, 9*(2), 191–204.

Hughes, P., and MacNaughton, G. (2000). *Building equitable staff-parent communication in early childhood settings: An Australian case study. Early Childhood Research & Practice,* 3(2).

Hutchinson, N. L., Pyle, A., Villeneuve, M., Dods, J., Dalton, C., and Minnes, P. (2014). Understanding parent advocacy during the transition to school of children with developmental disabilities: Three Canadian cases. *Early Years: An International Journal of Research and Development, 34*(4), 348–363. https://doi.org/10.1080/09575146 .2014.967662

Imray, P., and Colley, A. (2017). *Inclusion is dead: Long live inclusion.* Routledge.

Jalongo, M. R. (2002). On behalf of children: "Taking a stand: It is rocket science". *Early Childhood Education Journal, 30,* 65–66.

ISSA (2017). Webinar: Early childhood practitioners as advocates and activists. *YouTube.* https://www.youtube.com/watch?v=lETNLVl6jqQ

Jarman, E. (2007). Communication friendly spaces. In *Improving speaking and listening in the early.* Elizabeth Jarman Limited.

Jennings, P. A. (2015). Early childhood teachers' well-being, mindfulness, and self-compassion in relation to classroom quality and attitudes towards challenging students. *Mindfulness, 6*(4), 732–743.

Jeon, L., Buettner, C. K., and Grant, A. A. (2018). Early childhood teachers' psychological well-being: Exploring potential predictors of depression, stress, and emotional exhaustion. *Early Education and Development, 29*(1), 53–69.

Jessica A. Stern, Oscar Barbarin & Jude Cassidy (2021): Working toward anti-racist perspectives in attachment theory, research, and practice, *Attachment & Human Development,* DOI: 10.1080/14616734.2021.1976933

Kapp, S. K., Steward, R., Crane, L., Elliott, D., Elphick, C., Pellicano, E., and Russell, G. (2019). "People should be allowed to do what they like": Autistic adults' views and experiences of stimming. *Autism, 23*(7), 1782–1792.

Kessler, R. C., McLaughlin, K. A., Green, J. G., Gruber, M. J., Sampson, N. A., Zaslavsky, A. M., ... and Williams, D. R. (2010). Childhood adversities and adult psychopathology in the WHO World Mental Health Surveys. *The British Journal of Psychiatry, 197*(5), 378–385.

King, S., King, G., and Rosenbaum, P. (2004). Evaluating health service delivery to children with chronic conditions and their families: Development of a refined measure of processes of care (MPOC–20). *Children's Health Care, 33*(1), 35–57. https://doi.org/10 .1207/s15326888chc3301_3.

Kinman, G., Wray, S., and Strange, C. (2011). Emotional labour, burnout and job satisfaction in UK teachers: The role of workplace social support. *Educational Psychology, 31*(7), 843–856.

Korošec, H. (2012) Playing with puppets in class – Teaching and learning with pleasure. In: Kroßin, L., Ed., *The power of puppet*. The UNIMA Puppets in Education, Development and Therapy Commission.

Kranowitz, C. S. (2006). *The Out-of-Sync Child Has Fun: Activities for Kids with Sensory Processing Disorder*. Penguin.

Kranowitz, C. (2016). *The out-of-sync child grows up: Coping with sensory processing disorder in the adolescent and young adult years*. Penguin.

Lam, M. S., and Pollard, A. (2006). A conceptual framework for understanding children as agents in the transition from home to kindergarten. *Early Years, 26*(2): 123–141.

Lancet, T. (2020). Child mental health services in England: A continuing crisis. *The Lancet, 395*, (10222), 389.

Lansdown, G. (2005). *Can You Hear Me? The Right of Young Children to Participate in Decisions Affecting Them*. *Working Papers in Early Childhood Development, No. 36*. Bernard van Leer Foundation. PO Box 82334, 2508 EH, The Hague, The Netherlands.

Law, J., Charlton, J., and Asmussen, K. (2017). *Language as a child wellbeing indicator*. Early Intervention Foundation, Newcastle University.

Leedham, A., Thompson, A. R., Smith, R., and Freeth, M. (2020). "I was exhausted trying to figure it out": The experiences of females receiving an autism diagnosis in middle to late adulthood. *Autism, 24*(1), 135–146.

Lewis, A. (2019). Examining the concept of well-being and early childhood: Adopting multi-disciplinary perspectives. *Journal of Early Childhood Research, 17*(4), 294–308.

Lieberman, M. D., Eisenberger, N. I., Crockett, M. J., Tom, S. M., Pfeifer, J. H., and Way, B. M.. (2007). "Putting feelings into words. Affect labeling disrupts amygdala activity in response to affective stimuli." *Psychological Sciences, 18*(5): 421–428.

Light, R. (2003). The joy of learning: Emotion and learning in games through TGfU. *New Zealand Physical Educator, 36*(1), 93.

Lunn, N. (2021). *Conversations on love*. London: Penguin Books.

Macdonald, K., Germine, L., Anderson, A., Christodoulou, J., and McGrath, L. M. (2017). Dispelling the myth: Training in education or neuroscience decreases but does not eliminate beliefs in neuromyths. *Frontiers in Psychology, 8*, 1314.

Macvarish, J., Lee, E., and Lowe, P. (2014). The 'first three years' movement and the infant brain: A review of critiques. *Sociology Compass, 8*(6), 792–804.

Magda Quotes (n.d.). https://www.magdagerber.org/magda-quotes.html

Margetts, K. (2006). "Teachers should explain what they mean": What new children need to know about starting school. *Summary of paper presented at the EECERA 16th Annual Conference*, Reykjavik, Iceland.

Mashford-Scott, A., Church, A., and Tayler, C. (2012). Seeking children's perspectives on their wellbeing in early childhood settings. *International Journal of Early Childhood, 44*(3), 231–247.

McClelland, M. M., Cameron, C. E., Duncan, R., Bowles, R. P., Acock, A. C., Miao, A., and Pratt, M. E. (2007). Predictors of early growth in academic achievement: The head-toes-knees-shoulders task. *Frontiers in Psychology, 5*, 599.

McClelland, M. M., Cameron, C. E., Wanless, S. B., Murray, A., Saracho, O., and Spodek, B. (2007). Executive function, behavioral self-regulation, and social-emotional competence. *Contemporary Perspectives on Social Learning in Early Childhood Education, 1*, 113–137.

Mesibov, G. B., Shea, V., and Schopler, E. (with Adams, L., Burgess, S., Chapman, S. M., Merkler, E., Mosconi, M., Tanner, C., and Van Bourgondien, M. E.). (2005). *The TEACCH approach to autism spectrum disorders*. Springer.

Mheidly, N., Fares, M., Zalzale, H., and Fares, J. (2020). Effect of face masks on interpersonal communication during the COVID-19 pandemic. *Frontiers in Public Health, 8*, 582191.

Mitchell, L. M., and Philibert, D. B. (2002). Family, professional, and political advocacy: Rights and responsibilities. *Young Exceptional Children, 5*(4), 11–18.

Moriguchi, Y. (2014). The early development of executive function and its relation to social interaction: A brief review. *Frontiers in Psychology, 5*, 388.

Moriguchi, Y., and Hiraki, K. (2013). Prefrontal cortex and executive function in young children: A review of NIRS studies. *Frontiers in Human Neuroscience, 7*, 867.

Moriguchi, Y., Sakata, Y., Ishibashi, M., and Ishikawa, Y. (2015). Teaching others rule-use improves executive function and prefrontal activations in young children. *Frontiers in Psychology, 6*, 894.

Murray-Slutsky, C., and Paris, B. A. (2005). *Is it sensory or is it behavior: Behavior problem identification, assessment and intervention*. Hammill Institute on Disabilities.

Murray, D. W., Rosanbalm, K., Christopoulos, C., and Hamoudi, A. (2015). *Self-regulation and toxic stress: Foundations for understanding self-regulation from an applied developmental perspective*. (OPRE Report Number 2015-21).

My Feelings Colouring Chart (2021). http://www.socialworkerstoolbox.com/my-feelings-colouring-chart/

National Autistic Society (n.d.). Social stories and comic strip conversations. https://www.autism.org.uk/advice-and-guidance/topics/communication/communication-tools/social-stories-and-comic-strip-coversations

Neaum, S. (2019). *What comes before phonics?* SAGE.

Neaum, S. (2021). *What comes before phonics?*. SAGE.

Neuenschwander, R., Friedman-Krauss, A., Raver, C., and Blair, C. (2017). Teacher stress predicts child executive function: Moderation by school poverty. *Early Education and Development, 28*(7), 880–900.

NHS Digital (2016). Health Survey for England 2015 physical activity in children. http:// healthsurvey.hscic.gov.uk/media/37752/hse2015-child-phy-act.pdf

NHS Digital (2017/2020). https://digital.nhs.uk/data-and-information/publications/ statistical/mental-health-of-children-and-young-people-in-england/2020-wave-1-follow-up.

Nicholson, J., Driscoll, P. S., Kurtz, J., Marquez, D., and Wesley, L. (2020). *Culturally responsive self-care practices for early childhood educators*. Routledge.

Noddings, N. (2013). *Caring: A relational approach to ethics and moral education*. Univ of California Press.

Nutbrown, C., Clough, P., and Atherton, F. (2013). *Inclusion in the early years*. SAGE Publications Limited.

Oberklaid, F. (2020) Australia followed the science in managing COVID-19: We must do the same with early education. Women's Agenda. https://womensagenda.com.au/ latest/australia-followed-the-science-in-managing-covid-19-we-must-do-the-same -with-early-education/

Office for National Statistics https://www.ons.gov.uk/peoplepopulationandcommunity/ birthsdeathsandmarriages/deaths/articles/coronaviruscovid19relateddeathsbydisability statusenglandandwales/24januaryto20november2020.

Organisation for Economic Co-operation and Development Staff. (2002). *Education at a glance: OECD indicators 2002*. Paris: OECD.

Page, J., and Elfer, P. (2013). The emotional complexity of attachment interactions in nursery. *European Early Childhood Education Research Journal, 21*(4), 553–567.

Parker, M. N. (2020). *Educator wellbeing: Practical solutions to reset, recharge and recover*. Routledge.

Peters, S. A., and Paki, V. (2014). "They've definitely come a long; long way": The transformative possibilities of cross-sector collaboration. *24th EECERA Annual Conference*. Crete, Greece.

Pianta, R. C., Steinberg, M. S., and Rollins, K. B. (1995). The first two years of school: Teacher-child relationships and deflections in children's classroom adjustment. *Development and Psychopathology, 7*(2), 295–312.

Piggin, J. (2020). What is physical activity? A holistic definition for teachers, researchers and policy makers. *Frontiers in Sports and Active Living, 2,* 72.

Pineda-Alhucema, W., Aristizabal, E., Escudero-Cabarcas, J., Acosta-Lopez, J. E., and Vélez, J. I. (2018). Executive function and theory of mind in children with ADHD: A systematic review. *Neuropsychology Review, 28*(3), 341–358.

Pisaniello, S. L., Winefield, H. R., and Delfabbro, P. H. (2012). The influence of emotional labour and emotional work on the occupational health and wellbeing of South Australian hospital nurses. *Journal of Vocational Behavior, 80*(3), 579–591.

Pithouse, A., and Crowley, A. (2007). Adults rule? Children advocacy and complaints to social services. *Children and Society, 21,* 201–213.

Purdie, N., Carroll, A., and Roche, L. (2004). Parenting and adolescent self-regulation. *Journal of Adolescence, 27*(6), 663–676.

Rae, T., Cowell, N., and Field, L. (2017). Supporting teachers' well-being in the context of schools for children with social, emotional and behavioural difficulties. *Emotional and Behavioural Difficulties, 22*(3), 200–218.

Raghavan, R., and Alexandrova, A. (2015). Toward a theory of child well-being. *Social Indicators Research, 121*(3), 887–902.

Raikes, H. A., and Thompson, R. A. (2005). Efficacy and social support as predictors of parenting stress among families in poverty. *Infant Mental Health Journal: Official Publication of The World Association for Infant Mental Health, 26*(3), 177–190.

Rawstone, A. (2021). Early years staff struggling to support children's emotional and behavioural need. *Nursery World.* https://www.nurseryworld.co.uk/news/article/early -years-staff-struggling-to-support-children-s-emotional-and-behavioural-needs

Rimm-Kaufman, S. E., Pianta, R. C., and Cox, M. J. (2000). Teachers' judgments of problems in the transition to kindergarten. *Early Childhood Research Quarterly, 15*(2), 147–166.

Ring, E., Mhic Mhathuna, M., Moloney, M., Hayes, N., Stafford, P., Keegan, S.,... and Madden, R. (2016). *An examination of concepts of school readiness among parents and educators in Ireland.* Dublin: Department of Children and Youth Affairs. Available at: www.dcya.ie

Ring, E., and O'Sullivan, L. (2016). The importance of including the child's voice in the transition process. *Children's Research Network.* https://www.childrensresear chnetwork.org/knowledge/resources/the-importance-of-including-the-childs-voice-in -the-transition-process

Roberts, A., LoCasale-Crouch, J., Hamre, B., and DeCoster, J. (2016). Exploring teachers' depressive symptoms, interaction quality, and children's social-emotional development in Head Start. *Early Education and Development, 27*(5), 642–654.

Rosas, R., Espinoza, V., Porflitt, F., and Ceric, F. (2019). Executive functions can be improved in preschoolers through systematic playing in educational settings: Evidence from a longitudinal study. *Frontiers in Psychology, 10,* 2024.

Ryan, C., and Quinlan, E. (2018). Whoever shouts the loudest: Listening to parents of children with disabilities. *Journal of Applied Research in Intellectual Disabilities, 31*(Supplement 2), 203–214.

Sandberg, A., Lillvist, A., Eriksson, L., Björck-Åkesson, E., and Granlund, M. (2010). "Special support" in Preschools in Sweden: Preschool staff's definition of the construct. *International Journal of Disability, Development and Education, 57*(1), 43–57.

Sanders, M. R., Markie-Dadds, C., and Turner, K. M. (2003). *Theoretical, scientific and clinical foundations of the Triple P-Positive Parenting Program: A population approach to the promotion of parenting competence* (Vol. 1). Parenting and Family Support Centre, The University of Queensland.

Sanders, M. R., and Woolley, M. L. (2005). The relationship between maternal self-efficacy and parenting practices: Implications for parent training. *Child: Care, Health and Development, 31*(1), 65–73.

Sawyer, B. E., O'Connell, A., Bhaktha, N., Justice, L. M., Santoro, J. R., and Rhoad Drogalis, A. (2020). Does teachers' self-efficacy vary for different children? A study of early childhood special educators. *Topics in Early Childhood Special Education*, 0271121420906528.

Schaefer, P. S., Williams, C. C., Goodie, A. S., and Campbell, W. K. (2004). Overconfidence and the big five. *Journal of Research in Personality, 38*(5), 473–480.

Scholes, S., and Mindell, J. (2016). *Health survey for England 2015 physical activity in children.* NHS Digital.

Scionti, N., Cavallero, M., Zogmaister, C., and Marzocchi, G. M. (2020). Is cognitive training effective for improving executive functions in preschoolers? A systematic review and meta-analysis. *Frontiers in Psychology, 10,* 2812.

Seaman, H., and Giles, P. (2021). Supporting children's social and emotional well-being in the early years: An exploration of educators' perceptions. *Early Child Development and Care, 191*(6), 861–875.

Shonkoff, J. P., and Phillips, D. A. (Eds.). (2000). From neurons to neighborhoods: The science of early childhood development. Committee on Integrating the Science of Early Childhood Development, National Research Council and 20 Institute of Medicine. Washing.

Shonkoff, J. P., Garner, A. S., Siegel, B. S., Dobbins, M. I., Earls, M. F., McGuinn, L.,... and Committee on Early Childhood, Adoption, and Dependent Care. (2012). The lifelong effects of early childhood adversity and toxic stress. *Pediatrics, 129*(1), e232–e246.

Silkenbeumer, J., Schiller, E.-M., Holodynski, M., and Kärtner, J. (2016). "The role of co-regulation for the development of social-emotional competence." *Journal of Self-Regulation and Regulation, 2*(2): 17–32. https://doi.org/10.11588/josar.2016.2.34351.

Silkenbeumer, J. R., Schiller, E. M., and Kärtner, J. (2018). Co-and self-regulation of emotions in the preschool setting. *Early Childhood Research Quarterly, 44,* 72–81.

Souto-Manning, M., and Swick, K. J. (2006). Teachers' beliefs about parent and family involvement: Rethinking our family involvement paradigm. *Early Childhood Education Journal, 34*(2), 187–193.

Starr, E. M., Martini, T. S., and Kuo, B. C. H. (2014). Transition to kindergarten for children with autism spectrum disorder: A focus group study with ethnically diverse parents, teachers, and early intervention service providers. *Focus on Autism and Other Developmental Disabilities.* https://doi.org/10.1177/1088357614532497.

Steedman, C. (1990). *Childhood. Culture and class in Britain.* Virago.

Tedam, P. (2013). Understanding diversity, in T. Waller and G. Davis (eds.), *An introduction to early childhood.* 3rd edition. Sage.

Torrijos-Muelas, M., González-Víllora, S., and Bodoque-Osma, A. R. (2021). The persistence of neuromyths in the educational settings: A systematic review. *Frontiers in Psychology, 11,* 3658.

Trawick-Smith, J. (2019). *Young Children's Play: Development, Disabilities, and Diversity.* Routledge.

Trawick-Smith, J., and Dziurgot, T. (2010). Untangling teacher–child play interactions: Do teacher education and experience influence "Good-Fit" responses to Children's play? *Journal of Early Childhood Teacher Education, 31*(2), 106–128.

Tronick, E. Z. (2003). Things still to be done on the still-face effect. *Infancy, 4*(4), 475–482.

Understood (n.d.). For learning and thinking differences. https://www.understood
.org/Van der Kolk, B. (2014). *The body keeps the score: Mind, brain and body in the transformation of trauma.* Penguin UK.

Varese, F., Smeets, F., Drukker, M., Lieverse, R., Lataster, T., Viechtbauer, W.,... and Bentall, R. P. (2012). Childhood adversities increase the risk of psychosis: A meta-analysis of patient-control, prospective-and cross-sectional cohort studies. *Schizophrenia Bulletin, 38*(4), 661–671.

Vogler, P., Gina, C., and Woodhead, M. (2008). Early childhood transitions research: A review of concepts, theory, and practice. Working Paper 48.

Waters, S. F., West, T. V., and Mendes, W. B. (2014). Stress contagion: Physiological covariation between mothers and infants. *Psychological Science, 25*(4), 934–942.

Welsh, J. A., Nix, R. L., Blair, C., Bierman, K. L., and Nelson, K. E. (2010). The development of cognitive skills and gains in academic school readiness for children from low-income families. *Journal of Educational Psychology, 102*(1), 43.

Westling, D. L., Herzog, M. J., Cooper-Duffy, K., Prohn, K., and Ray, M. (2006). The teacher support program: A proposed resource for the special education profession and an initial validation. *Remedial and Special Education, 27*(3), 136–147. https://doi .org/10.1177/07419325060270030201.

White, S., and Abeyasekera, A. (2014). *Wellbeing and quality of life assessment: A practical guide.* Practical Action Publishing.

Whittaker, A. L., Lymn, K. A., Nicholson, A., and Howarth, G. S. (2015). The assessment of general well-being using spontaneous burrowing behaviour in a short-term model of chemotherapy-induced mucositis in the rat. *Laboratory Animals, 49*(1), 30–39.

Wolbring, G. (2008). The politics of ableism. *Development, 51*(2), 252–258.

Yates, T. M., Carlson, E. A., and Egeland, B. (2008). A prospective study of child maltreatment and self-injurious behavior in a community sample. *Development and Psychopathology, 20*(2), 651–671.

Zeanah, P. D., Stafford, B. S., Nagle, G. A., and Rice, T. (2005). *Addressing social-emotional development and infant mental health in early childhood systems. Building state early childhood comprehensive systems series, number 12.* UCLA Center for Healthier Children, Families and Communities.

Index

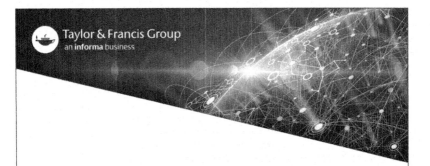